Milestones and Memories
A Century of Simcoe

Milestones and Memories

A Century of Simcoe

George E. Pond

Best Wishes
George Pond
Dec 1978

VOLUME I

The Norfolk Historical Society

Copyright © 1978, the Norfolk Historical Society

All rights reserved.
No part of this publication may be reproduced
without permission from the publishers.

ISBN 0-920624-00-6
Printed and bound in Canada

Design and graphic realization by Helmut W. Weyerstrahs

Typesetting by Compeer Typographic Services Limited
Printing and binding by The Hunter Rose Company

To my Mother and Father,
my wife Shirley and
our children Heather and David

Acknowledgements

The research for this book began prior to 1967, Canada's Centennial Year. Many hours were spent at that time collecting early photographs and postcards of Simcoe and searching through early issues of The Simcoe Reformer. Photo albums and slide presentations were prepared and displayed at the Eva Brook Donly Museum and various Centennial gatherings throughout that memorable year. Bruce Pearce, one of this area's most prominent historians who has published several historical books himself, was of tremendous help, especially in 1967, with his words of advice, his information and especially his encouragement.

In 1977 the decision was made to produce this book under the auspices of the Norfolk Historical Society. It is made possible by the generous assistance from the estate of the late John G. and Jessie Farrar.

We also thank The Simcoe Rotary Club for their financial assistance.

Hundreds of early photographs of Simcoe have been donated or loaned to me over the years by many interested and generous citizens of this community. In fact, new and exciting records of scenes and events of bygone years are still arriving on an almost weekly basis. To you people, whether or not your picture of Simcoe appears in this *Volume I*, must go the biggest "Thank You" of all. Individual photographs of our town are interesting and informative, collectively they tell an exciting pictorial story of the people, buildings and events that created our Town, Simcoe.

Thank you for sharing!

For historical information and/or photographs, in addition to the people mentioned above, I am indebted to: Victoria Barber, Bob Buck, George Brook, Lloyd S. Culver, Gordon ('Pat') Downs, Alice Gunton, Margaret Gunton, 'Alf' Johnson, Donna MacDonald, Douglas Nelles, Frank Peach, the late John Rutherford, Catharine Shaw, Helen Spencer, and Colonel Douglas Stalker.

Thanks, too, should go to Mr. Edward Phelps, Regional History Librarian, D. B. Weldon Library, University of Western Ontario; to Mr. David Judd of Simcoe who is himself preparing a very extensive history of this town through a Canada Works Project; to William Yeager, Curator of the Eva Brook Donly Museum, whose help in locating files, photos and negatives in the archives of the Norfolk Historical Society has been simply tremendous; and to the Publication Committee of the Norfolk Historical Society, Chris Lee and Harry Barrett, who have spent hours with the printers discussing and ironing out technical and financial details.

I am especially indebted to my former English teacher at Simcoe High School, Mr. Roger Booth, for editing my original manuscripts. He has unselfishly given many hours of time.

Thanks to my sales staff: Lil Tanchak, Duch Black, Keith Goble, Jim Learmonth, Pat Spencer and Marlene Smith for putting up with less than ideal working conditions these past many months.

My secretary, Carol Croucher, deserves special mention. Her willingness to work "over and above the call of duty" to meet publishing deadlines, helped make this book a reality during Simcoe's Centennial Year.

Appreciation is expressed to members of my own family: my mother, Bell Pond who spent hours deciphering and typing my scribbled notes and jumbled tape-recorded messages, and who wrote the poem "My Town — Simcoe" appearing in the Epilogue; my brother, Wilf Pond who sketched the line drawing of the Carillon Tower, his wife Bonnie Pond, my brother-in-law and sister, Don and Joan Daley and Mary Lee who helped with the eye-burning chore of proofreading the galley sheets; and finally, to my wife Shirley, my daughter Heather, and my son David, who helped with the final selection of photos for this book and who, for months, put up with early papers, photographs, historical pamphlets and books strewn throughout our home.

These acknowledgements would not be complete without special reference and thanks to the designer Helmut W. Weyerstrahs, of Toronto. It has been a pleasure and learning experience working with him.

Many photos and stories had to be deleted. Many more photos and postcards, long forgotten, are lurking in the attics of the older homes in town. Perhaps one day they will appear in Volume II of *Simcoe – Milestones and Memories*.

Contents

Introduction viii

Colborne Village to Lake George 2
    Old Windham Church, Air Line Station, Windham Mills,
    Cable's Carriage Works

Wellington Park to Downtown 18
    Kinsmen Park, Lake George, Simcoe High School,
    Carillon Tower, West & Peachey Foundry, Lynnwood Park

Downtown, Norfolk Street 35
    Duncan Campbell Estate, Falls Department Store,
    Norfolk Garage, Hendry & Walsh, Norfolk Hotel,
    Bank of Hamilton

East of Norfolk Street 85
    Lynnwood, Brookfield Arena, Mason Arena,
    Norfolk Golf & Country Club, Ritchie-Ford,
    Brook Woollen Company

Peel Street and Colborne Street 106
    The Old Post Office, Deans Hotel, Norfolk Country Court
    House, Hiller's Livery

Robinson Street 131
    Fireman's Arch, Melbourne Hotel, Battersby House,
    Simcoe Armouries, The Old Fire Hall, Simcoe Baptist
    Church, Simcoe Market

Simcoe West End 152
    Canadian Canners, The American Can Co., Simcoe
    Litho Company, Metcalfe Street Station, Union School,
    Norfolk General Hospital

South Simcoe 175
    Mason Brick Works, Norfolk County Fair, Brook's Dam

Dean Street to Downtown 182
    The Nelles Home, Methodist Church, Trinity Anglican Church,
    The Old Mud Church, St. Paul's Presbyterian Church

Epilogue 197

Introduction

Bird Town was the original name of the little community that stood at the headwaters of the Lynn River. However, in 1829 when the first Post Office was established, the name was changed to Simcoe — after the first Governor of Upper Canada, Colonel John Graves Simcoe.

Slowly the community grew, and foundries, gristmills, distilleries, carriage works, blacksmith shops, grocery stores and clothing shops were established to supply the needs of the surrounding farming community. In 1851, under the leadership of Nathan C. Ford, the first reeve, the town became incorporated as a village.

In 1878 the community had grown to a population of 2,000 and in that year with Dr. John Wilson as the first mayor, Simcoe became incorporated as a town.

This year, 1978, we celebrate that event with our 100th Anniversary. We have come a long way in the last one hundred years. We've grown from a population of a mere 2,000 to a sizeable community of some 14,000 people.

Our forefathers have planned well in the past. They have left us with a prosperous, friendly, beautiful community, truly southern Ontario's "Model Town". But what of the future? What lies ahead for this town, this Simcoe that we call "Home"?

The industrial expansion known as Nanticoke which is taking place south and east of Simcoe has brought with it predictions of a tremendous population increase for our area. New words and phrases have shown up in our daily vocabulary, expressions such as "Regional Government", "Nanticoke", "Stelco", "Satellite City", "Hydro", "O.M.B.", "Texaco", "New Town", "Townsend". They are words that to some spell progress and economic stability, a promise of greater income, of better and more exciting things to do. To others they spell concern and fear: fear that we are losing a way of life in this area, a way of life that developed at a slow and even rate over the past one hundred or more years, concern that we are losing a part of our heritage that has been handed down to us by our fathers and forefathers over the years.

It is not my intent to write about the pros and cons of these changes that are taking place. I would however like to go back in time with you and together we can look at some of the scenes and events of Simcoe in bygone years. Together we can catch a glimpse of the past. Perhaps we can gain some appreciation of the sweat and toil that has built this community. Perhaps we can gain some understanding of why those who have lived in Simcoe all their lives are concerned about the future, concerned that they may be losing a part of their heritage.

We will tour the town of "Yesterday" and see some of the achievements Simconians have made over the past years. Many of the buildings seen in our tour are gone now, victims of changing times and that greatest killer of all, fire. But some remain, reminders of the past, bridging the gap between then and now. These are sentinels guarding our heritage.

Our book is intended to give a pictorial glimpse into Simcoe's past, scenes of places and events of bygone days. It is not intended as a "people" history. Therefore I have made but sparing references to people, for many have played very prominent roles in the development of this community. Although it is hoped that this book will be used as a reference work, its main purpose is to give its readers an idea of the community life in our town over the years.

To enjoy the tour to the fullest, it is suggested that you actually take the trip through Simcoe past. The sequence of the pictures is such that you can drive, or, better still, walk through the town in the same order. Try to place yourself in the same position as the photographer when he took the picture. This will give you a better understanding of the exact location of the building or scene depicted and thus a better appreciation of the changes that have taken place over the years.

We will begin our trip in the north end of Simcoe and work our way down town. The various scenes that we will see were taken as early as 1860 and as recently as the 1940's. Many of the pictures are copies of photos, mostly originals, which have been given or loaned to me over the years by many interested people in Simcoe and Norfolk County. Others are copies of the vast photo collection contained in the archives of the Norfolk Historical Society; photos taken by some of Simcoe's most prominent early photographers — Isaac Horning, the Perry Bros., E. S. B. Moore and several others. Many of the more recent photos of Simcoe in my collection were taken over the past 25 or so years by Harold B. Stewart, one of our prominent local photographers. Space has limited the use of the more modern era, however a few of these photos appear, for which I am grateful.

Neither space nor time permits me to give a complete pictorial history of the downtown core section of Simcoe. The task of recording each and every tenant of each and every store would be an arduous one indeed. It would, however, be a worthwhile venture and I hope that someone with more patience than I, will eventually accomplish the task.

I have included in our tour many photos of downtown Simcoe taken at various times, from various locations, over the years. Some of our stores were occupied by the same tenants for fifty years or more, and reference is made to these establishments. Many however, were, as the saying goes, "here today and gone tomorrow". Other than the odd photo that may show a portion of their store front, there is little indication that they ever existed.

Then, too, many of the earlier prominent businesses were located in areas seldom photographed, such as the southerly end of the downtown section of Norfolk Street and all of Water Street running from Norfolk Street to the old Quance Mill property. There also does not appear to be much record by way of early pictures of Kent Street or Colborne Street South and I hope that somewhere in the attics and photo albums of the people of Norfolk, such photos will emerge and can be included in future photo records of our Town.

In order to "take you there" and to make the downtown scenes more meaningful, I have reproduced a few advertisements that appeared in early newspapers of many of the downtown stores and shops. I have also used a few reproductions of some of W. E. Cantelon's paintings of early Simcoe. These paintings show, in almost photographic exactness, many of the early buildings which once adorned our streets. We are fortunate indeed to have these paintings in our museum.

The information has been obtained by talking with many Simcoe and area residents and by searching through early copies of *The Norfolk Reformer*, *The British Canadian* and *The Simcoe Reformer*. I have also relied heavily on two fine books, both published by The Simcoe Reformer. One, *History of Simcoe 1829 to 1929* by Lewis Brown, and the other, *Simcoe and Norfolk County in Commemoration of the Reunion of Norfolk County Old Boys*, August 1924. I have tried to authenticate as much as possible the information which I have given to you in this book. However, some errors will come to light and for these I apologize.

George E. Pond
Simcoe, April 1978

Milestones and Memories
A Century of Simcoe

Old Windham Church

Old Windham Church has played a major role in the author's life. Therefore I have chosen the front of this long-gone landmark by the side of the road as the starting point of our trip "Down Memory Lane", our tour through Simcoe past.

This little church, the predecessor of the present modern Old Windham Church on Glendale Crescent, stood on the west side of No. 24 Highway, about two miles north of the present Norfolk Street North underpass. Its location is marked by a small memorial replica standing just north of the recently restored Old Windham Cemetery.

It was past this edifice that the Paris-Simcoe Stage Line would travel when making its daily trip to Simcoe during the 1800's and it was here that many of the early settlers and prominent citizens of Simcoe and Norfolk were laid to rest, each having played a part in the development of this fine community.

Old Windham Church dates back to 1794 when Reverend Jabez Culver, an ordained Presbyterian Minister, who had led a caravan of United Empire Loyalists to Norfolk County, began to preach in his log cabin home.

In 1820 a frame church was built south of the cabin. A brick structure was built in 1868 and called the "Windham Memorial Chapel of the New Connection Methodist Conference". This church was renovated in 1921 and a Sunday School addition was added in later years. The present new church was built in the early 1960's and was officially opened May 27, 1962.

The Old Windham Church Cemetery had been a "bone of contention" in the area for many years as seen in this article from the *British Canadian* on June 15, 1887:

"A visit to the Old Windham Cemetery will convince anyone that it is sadly neglected. Within its borders repose the ashes of some of the oldest settlers of this county, the pioneers of Ontario, and it is certainly not very creditable to see their graves overgrown with noxious weeds and many of the headstones standing in all sorts of shapes and some of them lying flat on the ground even. We hope someone will make a move to have its unsightly appearance remedied."

Similar articles appeared in other issues of local papers over the years. Finally in 1977 the old cemetery was cleaned up, the stones repaired and relocated on the same site in a more permanent and attractive setting.

Old Windham United Church, Colborne Village — circa 1925

The Air Line Station

Transportation was the life-stream of any early Canadian Town; Simcoe was no exception. Prior to the railway coming to Simcoe, goods and people were carried by stagecoach, one of the most popular being the Paris-Simcoe Stage Lines whose office was located on Peel Street

Railway was important talk as early as 1850 when at that time it was planned to run a Woodstock to Port Dover line. However, this never became a reality until 1875. Prior to that time, in 1872, the line of the Great Western Railway Air Line from Glencoe to Fort Erie reached Simcoe.

The original station, built in 1872, was about one hundred yards west of the present underpass on Norfolk Street, on the south side of the tracks. It was the site of a rather gala occasion when The Earl of Dufferin visited the town in 1874.

The *Simcoe Reformer* reported on Thursday, September 3, 1874: "The official train conveying the Vice-Regal Party arrived at the station on Friday last, punctually at the time named for its arrival. They were met by our County and Town officials, a guard of honor, the firemen and a large number of people. The passage from the train to the platform was very handsomely carpeted and furnished with easy chairs and sofas and decorated with evergreens. A beautiful arch with an appropriate motto spanned the entrance to the platform."

"Following this, the gathering formed into a procession and marched through the gaily decorated streets to the Court House, in front of which a dais with a canopy of evergreens had been erected."

"At the conclusion of this ceremony cheers were given for His Excellency and Lady Dufferin. The party was then driven to Lynnwood, the residence of Duncan Campbell Esq., who had invited their Excellencies to accept the hospitality of his house during his stay in town."

"The following morning the Vice-Regal Party visited the

Simcoe Station, Air Line Railway, on the occasion of the visit of His Excellency the Governor General to Simcoe, August 27, 1874. His Excellency is standing in front of the arch.

Union School where they were received by the children singing the National Anthem."

On October 27, 1904, the original station burned. Its fate and the story of the replacement was found in these articles from various issues of the *British Canadian*.

WEDNESDAY, NOVEMBER 2, 1904 — "The station in this town used jointly by the Wabash and Grand Trunk Railways was totally destroyed by fire on Thursday night. The fire originated in the north-west corner of the freight shed and spread so rapidly as to prevent the removal of the contents, only a small portion being saved. The fire spread to the station adjoining which was also destroyed but all the contents were removed. The station was so far distant from the firehall that the department could render but small service.

"It is stated that the company will at once rebuild a fine new modern structure. The business in the meantime will be carried on in temporary structures. The fire is suppose to have originated from a spark from a passing locomotive, fanned by a strong breeze."

NOVEMBER 16, 1904 — "Operations have commenced at the Air Line Station in this town for the erection of new freight sheds to take the place of those recently burned. We understand the new station is to be a modern frame one and if the weather keeps open will be built this fall."

JULY 19, 1905 — "The cement foundation for the new station at the Air Line is being put down. The station will be a very neat and convenient building and a credit to the town."

AUGUST 30, 1905 — "The new station at the Air Line is now so far advanced as to give a general idea of what it will be when completed. That it will be a fine looking and convenient structure is beyond question. It will be a credit to the town and the Railway Company. The new depot building came nearly to an untimely end on Monday afternoon. A live coal from a passing locomotive fell on the roof but was soon extinguished."

Air Line Station (looking West) — circa 1906

Both stations played an important part in the life of the people, and as trains came to town they would be met by horse-drawn buses from the Melbourne, Battersby and Norfolk Hotels.

The following articles were found in copies of the *British Canadian* of 1905:

JANUARY 4, 1905 — "The G.T.R.-Wabash are making some important changes in their water system at the Air Line Station. A new tank is being erected on the north side of the tracks. It will be put on iron pillars, twenty-one feet high. The staves of the tank will be sixteen feet high and the tank will be thirty-two feet in diamenter, having more than double the capacity of the old one. The tenders of the locomotives will be filled from two standpipes, one at the east end and one at the west end of the station yard. A large number of men are busily engaged in making the change."

APRIL 26, 1905 — "The Grand Trunk trainmen are getting indifferent to the convenience of the public. On Sunday a freight car was left standing across the sidewalk at the Union Street crossing to the inconvenience of those attending the Easter Services at St. Mary's Church. On Wednesday night a freight train was stretched across the Air Line crossing for twenty minutes with a large number of conveyances waiting to cross. The G.T.R. may own the Laurier Government but it has yet to purchase the Town of Simcoe."

The Air Line Station remained in service until July 1930 as seen in this headline from the *Simcoe Reformer*, July 17, 1930:

"AIR LINE STATION WIPED OUT BY DEVASTATING FIRE"

Apparently caused by a spark from a passing train, the Air Line Station was completely gutted by fire. A series of mishaps hampered the fire brigade and prevented the saving of the old landmark. In the first place, the fire brigade was misinformed and went to the Lake Erie and Northern Station where, of course, no fire was found. By the time they arrived at the fire and set up their hoses, it was discovered that there was not sufficient water pressure. No sooner was the water pressure corrected when one of the hose lines sprung a bad leak. By this time it was too late. A further catastrophe was averted when a gasoline train-car standing only some 500 feet from the inferno was pushed away by a group of bystanders.

CNR No. 88 and Water Tank — circa 1921

The Fire, July 17, 1930

Windham Mills

Windham Mills was the site of one of the first grist mills in Simcoe dating back to 1826. The original mill was built by William Wilson in 1826 and at that time a distillery formed part of the south end of the building. In 1874, William Sutton and D. Rose operated the grist mill as partners. The building burned in 1883 but was rebuilt the following year.

The photographer would be standing about the centre of the present bridge well up on Norfolk Street looking northwest.

On February 5, 1857 the following advertisement appeared in the *Conservative Standard*:

"GRISTING AT THE WINDHAM MILLS"

"The subscriber is now prepared to do all kinds of gristing work at the Windham Mills."

"Chopping and buckwheat grinding on Mondays and Saturdays. Cash for all kinds of grain."
Signed: J.G. Wilson, Simcoe

Following are some of the write-ups and advertisements that appeared in various issues of the *British Canadian*.
SEPTEMBER 7, 1881 — "Mr. William Sutton who has purchased the Windham Mills in this town, took possession on Monday."
MARCH 21, 1883 —

"DESTRUCTION OF
THE WINDHAM MILLS"
"We regret to announce that Mr. William Sutton's mills near the Air Line Railway Station in the North Ward were entirely destroyed by fire Monday afternoon. The loss to Mr. Sutton who has proved to be an energetic and enterprising man will be serious as only last fall he expended a large sum of money in renewing the flume and putting new machinery in the mill. We hope that Mr. Sutton will be able to replace it at as early a date as possible."
JUNE 26, 1889 — "Mr. William Sutton is having his dam at the Windham Mills piled. We hope he will succeed in making a dam that will withstand the freshets."
OCTOBER 30, 1901 —

"*Windham Mills*"
"Choice Manchester Wheat wanted at 68¢; White Wheat 65¢; Oats wanted at 37¢. All other coarse grain highest market price. Flours $1.50 and $1.75; Chop $1.10; Grain 85¢; Middlings $1.00; Buckwheat 50¢. All guaranteed first class or money refunded."
Signed: William Sutton

Windham Mills, Norfolk Street North, Simcoe — circa 1900

Polley's General Store, south-west corner of Colborne & Main Streets — circa 1927

Polley's General Store

Miss Polley's General Store stood facing Colborne Street North on the south-west corner of Main and Colborne Streets. The store stood here for many years and was removed about 1927, to make way for the erection of the North Public School.

Polley's Foundry was located behind the store on the north side of Windham Street, just to the rear of the present North School.

The Foundry was built by John Polley about 1837 and for some 40 years was a thriving industry in Simcoe. The Polley Plough, patented by Mr. Polley, was considered one of the finest in the country.

In the *British Canadian* of June 12, 1889

there is an article about a fire in the two-storey frame building situated in the North Ward almost opposite Polley's Store. The burned building was for many years used as a fanning mill factory.

Wellington Heights Army Camp

During the Second World War, 1939-45, an army training centre known as No. 25 C.I.B.T.C. was located in what is now Simcoe's Wellington Heights' Industrial Park. Many of the war time barracks are still in existence, converted to warehouses, workshops, office and a dance studio.

This photograph, showing the Officer's Mess, was taken circa 1943.

The Erie Fire Company

At one time the Simcoe Fire Companies consisted of two separate companies, No. 1 Company and The North Ward or "Wellington Brigade". No. 1 Company had its fire department on The Market Square, while the fire house of The Wellington Brigade was located on the south side of Windham Street about halfway between Colborne and Talbot Streets, just south of the present North School building. Many years ago this building was sold by the town and has since been used for residential purposes.

A few paragraphs from Lewis Brown's *History of Simcoe 1829-1929* give the following account:

"After the new engine was installed, the old "cataract" which had done service for more than 25 years, was, at the suggestion of Councillor Coates, taken to the North Ward, overhauled and the poles on either side lengthened so as to accommodate three added men each to increase the power. A frame building was erected as shelter and a comfortable hall upstairs for a meeting place. This was the Alpha of the North Ward Fire Company and as it turned out, although they had only the old engine, they "cut some ice". We don't mean on Sutton's pond, but at the fire when there was one downtown."

"There was many a race between Number 1 and Number 2, and although Number 1 had the best of it for distance it was not at all infrequent for Number 2 to head them off. Too much praise cannot be given our North Ward Fire Brigade for all these fifty-odd years. When there was something doing they were ever "Johnny on the job."

The Erie Fire Company, Windham Street — circa 1920

Cable's Bridge — circa 1860

Cable's Bridge, Paris Stage and Kent Brewery

The photographer, standing about sixty yards south of the present concrete bridge on Colborne Street North, facing northwest, took this picture of a thriving complex of mid nineteenth century industry.

Jutting into the skyline is the angular roof of the old Polley Foundry.

"Cable's Bridge" got its name from its proximity to Cable's Carriage Works. The carriage works was to the right of the photographer.

Parallel to the main bridge was a foot-bridge, which, on May 11, 1870 was to arouse the ire of the *Norfolk Reformer*:

"THE SIDEWALKS"

"We hear frequent complaints about the condition of the sidewalks which are in a sad state of repair in many places. It is about time too, that the foot-bridge on Colborne Street which was washed away in the spring, be rebuilt."

Between the foot bridge and the main bridge there was a ford which not only provided a watering place for the horses but also ensured that the Daily Mail Stage coach could always get through. The photographer has caught in his camera the coach crossing Cable's Bridge on its way to/from Paris on one of its daily runs.

This pioneer transportation firm advertised its services in *The Erie News* and *Norfolk Reformer*, March 1, 1860:

"Daily Mail Stage to Brantford and Paris from Simcoe running in conjunction with the Great Western and Buffalo and Lake Huron Railways. Mail Stage leaves Simcoe every evening, Sundays excepted at six o'clock for Brantford and Paris, returning it leaves Paris at nine o'clock p.m. This line will run punctually to time, four hours between Simcoe and Brantford. Covered coaches, good buffalo robes, sober drivers and every comfort to passengers. Express parcels carried with all safety."

J. Hill, Proprietor.

The buildings in the far right background are probably those of the Gibbon and Evans Soap Factory which advertised in the *British Canadian*, April 6, 1887:

"SOAP & ICE"

"Gibbon and Evans beg to announce that they will constantly keep on hand a stock of soap at the Gibbon Factory in the North Ward and will make a specialty of Gibbon's famous labour-saving soap. Will exchange soap for ashes and grease. Have stored a large supply of excellent ice which they will deliver during the coming season in quantitites to suit customers."

The building on the left in the picture is rather like Old Sila's jack-knife, his "one-and-only", as he said, which he had treasured from his tenth birthday to his death sixty years later though it had had "three new blades and two new handles" in that time. Edwin B. Kent had built it to house his Brewery which became the principal dispensary of beer in this district from about 1840 to 1880.

The following ad appeared in O.L. Fuller Business Directory, 1865 and 1866 for Norfolk County:

"EDWIN P. KENT, BREWER,
Colborne St., Upper Town,
Simcoe, Canada West"

"Hotels and families supplied with ale, porter and beer in casks or bottles on reasonable terms."

It was in 1880 that Mr. H.D. Finlay took over the Kent Brewery. Mr. Finlay operated it for about six years before he closed it down.

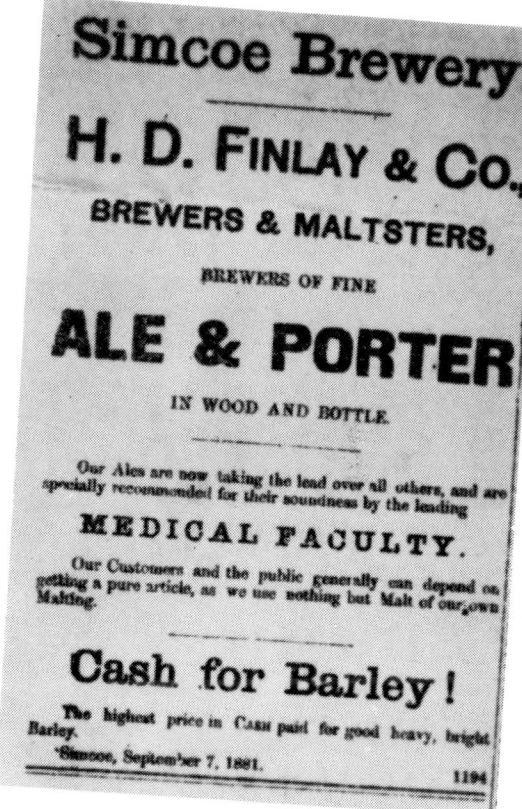

*W. F. Steinhoff Foundry & Machine Shop.
Photo by E. S. B. Moore — circa 1903*

In 1890 Mr. W. F. Steinhoff converted the building into a machine shop and operated it until his death.

The *British Canadian* ran this notice on June 25, 1890:

"W. F. Steinhoff has erected a shop on the old brewery site on Colborne Street and is manufacturing windmills. He has just completed a number and they work like a charm. Farmers are adopting these labour-saving machines for pumping water for stock, etc., and anyone wanting one should call Mr. Steinhoff. Farmers are invited to inspect the workings of his windmills."

Then it ran this news item January 22, 1902:

"ANOTHER FIRE"
"About half-past nine last Thursday forenoon, smoke was observed issuing from the roof of Mr. W. Findley Steinhoff's Foundry on Colborne Street in the North Ward. An alarm was sent in and both steamers were sent out. Immense volumes of smoke issued from the building and it looked at one time as if the structure was doomed."

It was in 1904 that Mr. John Stalker took over the machine shop and foundry. Mindful of Steinhoff's experience with fires, he, during the following twenty years replaced all the original frame portions of the buildings with a brick structure.

During the First World War, the enterprising owner ran this advertisement in the *Simcoe Reformer* on December 13, 1917:

"Right Now! Look after your storage battery. We are equipped to re-charge, repair, overhaul and winter-store all types and makes of batteries."

"The Ever Ready Service Station."
Signed: J. M. Stalker,
            250-260 Colborne Street N.

The building, now known as Stalker Engineering Company is owned by John's son, Colonel Douglas Stalker.

Cable's Carriage Works

Cable's Carriage Works stood on the east side of Colborne Street, just at the foot of Maple Street. The land is now covered by 205 and 211 Colborne Street North. The photographer would be standing just east of the present Colborne Street bridge looking south. This was a busy carriage building factory employing many hands in the 1850's and 1860's.

From the *Long Point Advocate*, August 11, 1851, the following ad:

"NEW FIRM, CARRIAGE MAKING, BLACKSMITHING, ETC. ETC."
"Mr. John W. Cable begs to return his sincere thanks to the public for the liberal patronage bestowed upon the late firm of Cable, Cable & Dill and to inform the inhabitants of Norfolk that having formally formed a co-partnership with his brother, Mr. James Cable, carriage maker, they are now prepared to do all kinds of work in their line on the shortest notice and most reasonable terms."

"The greatest attention will be paid to horseshoeing by Mr. J. W. Cable who has no doubt of giving general satisfaction in that part of his business. Also jobbing of all kinds expeditiously and cheaply executed."
Signed: J.W. & J. Cable, Simcoe
April 12, 1851

Cable's Carriage Works, Colborne Street N. — circa 1852

Colborne Street Bridge

The photographer was standing south of the Colborne Street Bridge looking north. Notice the change in the foot bridge since the early days of 1860. The Stalker Engineering building on the left across the bridge is obscured by the trees.

Lake George in the early days was called Crystal Lake as seen in this write-up from the *British Canadian*, July 6, 1887. The article is about Simcoe's Jubilation on July 1st and talks about the bands and parades etc. that took part on the holiday.

...."Twenty years ago last Friday, The Dominion of Canada was born"....

"At eight o'clock the firemen assembled at the central firehall and formed a torchlight procession which, headed by the band, marched through some of the principal streets to the park at Crystal Lake where a vast concourse of people were assembled to witness the display of fireworks. Whether the people expected too much, or the fireworks were inferior, or the moon was too bright, or the hotentot weather was to blame, deponents saith not but the fact cannot be disguised that the display did not meet the expectations of many and caused a good deal of grumbling."

"We are pleased to say that with the exception of the collapse of a portion of the foot bridge over Kent's Creek which luckily did not result in injury to any person, no accidents occurred during the day and evening and we believe that people returned to their homes well pleased with Simcoe jollification."

Colborne Street North Bridge and Lake George — circa 1910

The Lawn Bowling Club

Simcoe's original Lawn Bowling Greens — circa 1907

The original Lawn Bowling Club was located on the north-east corner of Colborne and Union Streets adjacent to the Curling Club, in the same location as the present Lutheran Church.

The Curling Club walls can be seen in the background with a sign advertising one of Simcoe's many livery stables.

Previous to the Curling Rink being built, the townspeople curled on Crystal Lake. As we learn from the *British Canadian*, January 11, 1888:
"The first game of curling of the season took place on Crystal Lake last Wednesday between two local rinks. The ice was very good and the play keen as will be seen by the following score: J. C. Boyd, skip, 19; G. A. Curtis, skip, 14."

On Wednesday, September 30, 1896, the *British Canadian* reported: "Contractor Rattenbury has commenced operations on the large Curling Rink to be erected on the corner of Colborne and Union Streets opposite Devall's Factory."

The Curling Club was ready on November 15, 1896.

Across the street on the north-west corner of Union and Colborne Streets, there used to be a Planing Mill, which was destroyed by fire. The *British Canadian*, September 14, 1895 reported: "Devall's Factory burned. On Monday night between ten and eleven o'clock, James Devall's Factory and Planing Mill, which was situated on the corner of Colborne and Union Streets, together with its valuable contents of machinery, lumber and uncompleted work was destroyed by fire."

Wellington Park

Wellington Park — circa 1950

Simcoe's main softball diamond was located in Wellington Park from the 1930's to 1967 when Centennial Park was established. The lighted diamond above was considered by many ball players as one of the finest in Southern Ontario. Many local ball fans have fond memories of exciting games; both ladies and men played here during the depression and war years.

The photographer was standing about 100 feet west of Norfolk Street, half-way between Bonnie Drive and Windham Streets, looking south-west. Home plate was located in the south-west corner of the present park.

Simcoe Chamber of Commerce "Christmas Panorama" — circa 1965

The Simcoe Panorama Display, located in the Wellington and Clifton Park areas began in 1958 with six displays. By 1977 there were over sixty displays depicting fantasies, religious and Christmas scenes. In 1976 an estimated 250,000 people visited the display during December.

This view of the lighted tree and boat in Lake George is from the west bank of the lake along Kent Street, looking north-east.

Kinsmen Park

One of the first projects of the Simcoe Kinsmen Club which was organized in 1927, was the establishment of the Kinsmen Park and Children's Playground. The park was on Lake George between the two Norfolk Street Bridges. Swings, teetertotters, sandboxes and other recreational facilities were provided for the children, as well as a sandy swimming area. Many a Simcoe resident can remember as a child jumping into the water from the arched wooden bridge which connected the mainland to the small island.

The photograph was taken from the west side of Norfolk Street, looking north-westerly — circa 1945.

Lake George

Lake George from Bonnie Drive — circa 1950. Notice the Lawn Bowling Club which was established here in 1945. The West & Peachey Foundry was torn down in 1953. The white concrete bridge was replaced on October 29, 1958, by a concrete and steel bridge.

Lake George from Bonnie Drive — circa 1965. Notice the rocks and fence around the lighthouse which was erected by The Simcoe Lions Club in 1964 and the beautification program which has taken place around the banks of the lake. Bonnie Drive was curbed in 1963. The Post Office in the back right hand corner was completed in 1955.

Simcoe High School

Left: Simcoe High School — circa 1908. Seen from south shore of River Lynn, just east of bridge, looking north-east.

Right: Science Room, Simcoe High School. This photo was taken by Mr. E. S. B. Moore, local photographer, on March 26, 1908. It was ordered by the Principal, Mr. J. D. Christie.

The original Simcoe High School was built in 1893 where formerly the residence of Mr. Edward Freeman stood. The High School was in the same location as the present Simcoe Composite School, however none of the original building remains.

The first principal was J. D. Christie, B.A., who remained as principal until 1921 when James E. Skeel, B.A., succeeded him. The High School was officially opened in 1894.

The completion of the High School relieved the congestion from The Union (or Central School) which was located on Metcalfe Street.

Simcoe High School — circa 1906, looking east from about the site of the present Carillon Tower. Notice the flagstaff to the north of the school, which is mentioned in the British Canadian, *May 27, 1903: "Last Wednesday afternoon the grounds at the High School had an animated appearance. The cause was the unfurling of a large Canadian Flag on the high steel flagstaff which had just been erected."*

Girl's P.T. Class, lined up for a physical education class — circa 1905

These two photographs were taken in 1931 from the Carillon Tower looking east. In the top photo the excavation has just taken place to the north of the High School for the new gymnasium and auditorium (now the old gymnasium and auditorium). The two rooms at the south end had been added in 1924. The middle photo shows the 1931 addition half completed. It was opened in 1935. In 1939 another six-room addition was built. Notice the area behind the High School; this is the present Country Club, Basil Avenue, Lynndale Road, Ormond Crescent, Simcoe Boulevard area.

Simcoe High School, from the south side of the Carillon Tower looking east — circa 1946

Aerial View of Simcoe High School, Carillon Tower and Lake George area — circa 1957. Notice: The Post Office, dedicated July 1955; Lawn Bowling Club, established here in 1945; White Concrete Bridge, replaced in 1958; Carillon Tower, dedicated June 1925; High School before addition of 1959.

Simcoe Carillon Tower

Norfolk's War Memorial was dedicated on June 17th, 1925. The structure is 60 feet in height by 22 feet square. It is constructed of Hagersville limestone and trimmed with carved Indianna stone and is set on a pile foundation.

The carillon comprises 23 bells weighing over 8,000 pounds.

Located on the south-east corner of Norfolk Street and Wilson Avenue, the Carillon was erected to commemorate the gallant sons of Norfolk who paid the supreme sacrifice on the battlefields of France during the First World War.

In 1946, after the 2nd World War, 1939-45, a suitable plaque was added to the tower in honour of those brave servicemen who paid the supreme sacrifice.

Photographed circa 1940.

Kinsmen Club Swimming Pool

The pool was located at the back of the present Composite School building in about the same location as the greenhouse. It was constructed and donated to the Town of Simcoe in 1938 by the Simcoe Kinsmen at a cost of $12,000. It operated in this location until 1960 when it was levelled to make way for an addition to the High School.

It was replaced by the present modern pool on Windham Street at a cost of approximately $122,000 and donated to the Town by the Kinsmen Club of Simcoe in 1961.

In the top photo, taken circa 1940, the photographer was standing at the bend in the river behind the High School looking south. The Argyle Street bridge and chimney from the Brook Woollen Company can be seen in the background.

The photo at the bottom was taken circa 1950 from the south-east corner of the pool looking westerly. Change rooms were in the background. The trees were located along the north bank of the Lynn River between the river and the High School.

West, Peachey & Sons Foundry — circa 1950

West, Peachey & Sons Foundry

Established in 1878 by James Peachey and John West on the north-west corner of Colborne and Young Streets. The business flourished so quickly that by 1879 they purchased the property on the north-west corner of Norfolk and Union Streets where the present Post Office is now situated. A foundry building was erected and the business remained at this location until 1953 when the old foundry was demolished to make way for the new Federal Building.

The West Machinery business was moved to a new location in Wellington Heights, Simcoe's then new Industrial Park.

The above picture was taken shortly before the old foundry disappeared. It was at this location that the famous "Alligator" steam warping tugs were manufactured.

On October 24, 1883, the *British Canadian* wrote:

"DESTRUCTIVE FIRE"

"We regret to announce that Messrs. West and Peachey's Foundry in this town was almost totally destroyed by fire last Thursday night, and what was before a busy scene of industry is now a smouldering ruin. About eleven o'clock flames were discovered issuing from the roof at the west end of the building by the family of Mr. Mel Dean who gave the alarm."

The building shown in our photo replaced the burned-out structure shortly after the fire.

The Centennial edition of the *Simcoe Reformer*, June 3, 1967, had the following article about the West and Peachey Alligator Tug:

"ALLIGATOR TUG IS JACK OF ALL TRADES"

"Mr. West devised the alligator which could run on land or water and in 1889 a trial order for the first alligator steam warping tug was filled."

"For a quarter of a century the building of the alligator was the firm's principal trade brought with the cleaning up of the Northern Ontario timber and the slackening of rafting and the installation of local mills, the alligator became a necessary commodity. Production of the tug ceased in 1932."

The following description of the alligator steam warping tugs invented and produced in Simcoe by West & Peachey was taken from a calendar apparently used from 1903 to 1906 as an advertising media by the firm:

"Lumbering operations have of late years been driven back so far amongst ranges of small lakes connected by narrow and uncertain outlets that it has become a serious question to many lumbermen how to get their timber and logs over these lakes and outlets during the short season of high water. The old horse capstan has been found to be too slow besides being awkward and involving much labour and loss of time in moving it from place to place."

"We take much pleasure in introducing to lumbermen and mill owners our invention which is intended to take the place of the capstan, and which we have patented in Canada and the United States. We call it the Alligator or Warping Tug. It has been in successful operation since 1889 on the Northern Lakes and Rivers."

"It will climb hills and go through swamps, or up small streams from one lake to another. After warping down a boom of logs it will return with an empty boom, doing the work cheaply and thoroughly with a great saving of time and of number of men."

When not being used in the water as a tug boat, the machine was capable of pulling itself across the land by use of mile-long steel cables. Thus, the boat was

Early "Side Paddler" Steam Warping Tug — circa 1901. The original tugs were side paddlers. The above christened "Victoria" is in the Lynn River east of the long bridge on Norfolk Street. The original high school completed in 1894, is in the background.

"W.T. WHITE" Alligator No. 39 — circa 1898, floating in Lake George (then Crystal Lake), on the west side of Norfolk Street. The old long bridge, a wooden structure, can be seen behind the tug as can the original high school building east of the bridge. The photographer was probably on the grounds of the West and Peachey Foundry.

West & Peachey Steam Warping Tug — circa 1920. The tug is going down the Lynn River to the train station at the Lake Erie and Northern Railway located at the foot of the Argyle Street Bridge.

Alligator Tugs in River Lynn — circa 1920. Looking south from the north bank of the Lynn River east of the Norfolk Street Bridge. Lynnwood Park can be seen beyond the Tugs and in the far background the Lynnwood Survey.

a great boon in the lumbering industry for many years. The largest of these tugs was used in the jungles of the Amazon.

There is still a Steam Warping Alligator Tug on view in a logging display in Algonquin Park.

Many reports appear in early Simcoe papers relating to the steam warping tugs of Simcoe.

In the *British Canadian*, June 26th, 1895, a story entitled "Killed By An Alligator", talked about the Alligators of West & Peachey up at Parry Sound. Apparently a workman was killed during logging operations, thus, the strange heading.

On May 1, 1901 the *British Canadian* reports:

"Messrs. West & Peachey shipped on Thursday, the Alligator Warping Tug "Victoria" to Callender, Lake Nipissing. It was built for the Victoria Lumber Company who carry on an extensive business in that district. This is the 46th boat built by Messrs. West & Peachey and the sixth one built by them since January 1st. We are pleased with the success of this enterprising firm."

The following news item appeared in the *British Canadian* on April 29, 1903: "On Thursday, Messrs. West & Peachey shipped an Alligator Warping Tug to the Shepherd & Morris Lumber Company, Temiskaming, Quebec. It was named "The Pontiac" and is the 53rd boat built by the firm."

Lynnwood Park — circa 1910, looking north from Lynnwood Avenue, just east of Norfolk Street.

Lynnwood Park

In 1795, it is said that John Graves Simcoe, first Lieutenant-Governor of Upper Canada, stopped to rest upon the banks of the River Lynn on the site which is now Lynnwood Park.

Another story is told that this park many years ago was an Indian camping ground, having somewhere near the centre, a depression where the fires were kept burning.

The park was once part of the property of Duncan Campbell, Simcoe's first Postmaster, and was presented to the Town in 1903 by his son, J. Lorne Campbell, a prominent citizen and ex-Mayor.

The gift of Lynnwood Park to the Town on the occasion of the 1903 Victoria Day Celebration created quite a stir within the community.

The *Simcoe Reformer*, May 1903 reported the event as follows:
"Victoria Day right royally celebrated by Norfolk people in their County Town. Lynnwood Park formally dedicated with appropriate ceremony for the use, for all time to come, of our citizens and neighbours. Large crowds of visitors invade the town. Everything passes off without a hitch. Delightful weather, inspiring speeches, a fine program of sports, winding up at night with a beautiful illumination and a clever minstrel performance combined to fill a long and pleasant holiday."

And on May 27, 1903 the *British Canadian* wrote:
"VICTORIA DAY IN SIMCOE GRAND CELEBRATION"
"The celebration of Victoria Day in this town last Monday may very probably be called the premier celebration ever held. The weather was delightfully cool and the thousands of visitors who came to town to participate in the joyousness of the day were certainly rewarded for their visit. The greatest event on the program was the dedication of the handsome park presented to the town by the ex-mayor, J. Lorne Campbell; and the thousands who visited this picturesque spot were unstinted in their praise of the donor of the noble gift."

Lynnwood Park — circa 1940

Snow Scene, Lynnwood, Park — circa 1910, looking east from Norfolk Street. Notice the many benches scattered throughout the park.

Looking south along the east side of Norfolk Street Bridge from the Carillon Tower. This concrete bridge replaced the old wooden bridge referred to in the following article in the *British Canadian*, May 18th 1887:

"The new bridge that spans the Lynn on Norfolk Street was the scene of quite a flutter on Saturday evening when the imposing ceremony of christening it was performed by Squire Freeman in the presence of a goodly number of our townspeople. It was named Victoria Bridge in honour of Her Majesty's Jubilee."

"During the evening excursions were given on Crystal Lake by the *Little Gem* under the command of Captain Peachey, which were enjoyed by a large number of ladies and gentlemen. We noticed that the tidy little craft has been refitted and repainted and looks quite nobly."

Duncan Campbell Estate, from Norfolk Street — circa 1895

The Duncan Campbell Estate

The above photo, taken by the late John Rutherford around the turn of the century, is one of the few pictures left that gives one an idea of the beauty and spaciousness of this huge estate which stood in the heart of town.

The fence ran from the Argyle Street bridge west along Argyle Street to the Norfolk Street corner and then north along Norfolk Street to approximately the corner of Lynnwood Park. The park at that time was owned by Duncan Campbell and was left in a wilderness state. It was completely fenced in and contained a few deer which were always of interest to the youth of the day.

Many rare plants could be found on the estate, as we learn from the *British Canadian*, June 19, 1878:

"SOMETHING RARE"

"D. Campbell Esq., has in his grounds a tulip tree in blossom. These are very rare. There are very few of these trees in Canada not another, we believe, in the county. This is the second time it has flowered."

The Post Office — circa 1850, from a painting by W.E. Cantelon.

In 1829 Duncan Campbell was appointed Postmaster of Simcoe's newly formed Post Office. He built this little white cottage on the north-east corner of Argyle and Norfolk Streets. The building faced Argyle Street and stood here until close to the close of the century. It once housed the Gore Bank and later, when Mr. Campbell became a "Gentleman's Businessman", it became his own personal office. The building was moved to its present location at 76 Kent Street South and is now the office of The Simcoe Chamber of Commerce.

From the *Norfolk Observer*, Saturday, April 17th, 1841, the following ad:

"NOTICE — The highest rate of exchange will be paid for bills on England, Ireland and Scotland. Drafts on Montreal, or any other part of the Canadas, and the United States, will be cashed at the subscriber's office, No. 4, Norfolk Street, Simcoe."

Signed: Duncan Campbell, Agent for the Gore Bank

In the *British Canadian*, Wednesday, March 29, 1893 we find this notice: "Tenders will be received by the undersigned up to the 5th of April next for the old Gore Bank building at the corner of Norfolk and Argyle Streets. The foundation is of brick and stone. The building contains a good brick vault with iron doors. The whole is to be removed by the 30th of April next. The lowest or any tender not necessarily accepted. The office furniture including a second-hand safe will be disposed of by private sale."
                                                              Duncan Campbell

Taken by John Rutherford, this photo clearly shows the wilderness condition of The Duncan Campbell Estate. The photo was taken sometime after the little white Post Office building was moved in 1893.

East Side of Norfolk Street North — circa 1900

The photographer was standing on the east side of Norfolk Street approximately at the Norfolk Street/Young Street corner. The photo is taken looking north along the fence in front of the Duncan Campbell Estate.

A few years after this photo was taken, the old fence along Norfolk Street was torn down and a sidewalk was laid all the way to the bridge. By 1907 the Lynnwood area was being developed and houses and stores began to appear on the scene.

The following article appeared in the *British Canadian*, April 22, 1903:

"The fence in front of the new park has been removed and the handsome grounds are being got in order. The lower portion is being tile-drained and stumps are being removed. A granolithic walk will be put in front of the park; a bandstand is to be erected and conveniences for picnic parties are to be added. Simcoe has every reason to be proud of the handsome gift made by Mr. Campbell."

Building of Falls Department Store — circa 1912

H.S. Falls Department Store

In 1877 Harvey Falls entered the Golden Bee Hive Store of Oscar Hendry as an apprentice at the age of 17, the year before the incorporation of the Town of Simcoe.

For years, Ritchie, Ford & Company had conducted a general store on the site of the Willis Kindy store of today. In 1874, fire destroyed the premises and the firm moved to the Victoria Block now occupied

Grand Opening, H.S. Falls Department Store

Interior of Falls Department Store — circa 1915. Notice the prices: dustcaps 9¢; aprons 19¢; bungalo aprons 39¢; polish mops 53¢.

by the F.W. Woolworth Company. The junior partner, N.C. Ford became owner in due course and was succeeded by George J. McKiee in 1891. The latter gave up business and Northway and Anderson purchased stock and goodwill, and in December of that year, young Harvey Falls became a partner. Eventually he became manager and later, proprietor.

By 1912 the old store was decidedly cramped and that year the fine new block across the street was erected. The new store was on the site of the Duncan Campbell Estate, where the first Simcoe Post Office stood in 1829. Customer satisfaction and shopping comfort was of prime concern to Mr. Falls. An hydraulic elevator was installed much to the pleasure of the townspeople and on the second floor a waiting room and comfortable rest rooms had been built for extra special comfort.

The Falls Store measured 80' × 105'. A large write-up in the *Simcoe Reformer* on November 21st, 1912, stated: "The realization of an ideal; here it stands, almost complete inside and out." This three-storey building was for years one of the most modern department stores in southern Ontario. It was burned in 1937.

The Falls fire of that February night is still remembered by many as one of the most devastating and intense infernos ever to take place in downtown Simcoe.

Interior of Falls Department Store — circa 1915, then considered one of the most modern stores in Ontario.

Falls Department Store Fire, Feb. 13, 1937

Erection of Roy W. Wallace Block, 11-15 Norfolk Street North — circa 1910

The Roy W. Wallace Building

The Roy W. Wallace building originally contained a dance hall on the second floor which has since been converted to apartments.

In 1914 Mr. Wallace was given the franchise to sell Ford cars and a garage remained here for many years. Now it is a music store, real estate office and variety shop. The photo on the right shows a delivery of Model "T" Fords to the R.W. Wallace Ford Garage. Notice the sign in the street "Ford Delivery from Port Rowan". The photo also shows the location of the Reformer Offices north of the garage. The photographer was looking north along the east side of Norfolk Street.

The following ad appeared in the *Simcoe Reformer* on July 31, 1924, on the occasion of the Simcoe Old Boy's Reunion:
"Old boys and girls, bring your car troubles to Norfolk Garage next to Falls Store. Experienced mechanics and adequate equipment enable us to render an unusual service."
Lorne Walker, Manager

Norfolk Garage — circa 1914

Circus Parade on Norfolk Street — May 24, 1912

Downtown — West Side of Norfolk Street

The photo on the left page was taken by John Rutherford while standing on the roof of the Falls Store on the north-east corner of Argyle and Norfolk Streets. Falls was still under construction at the time. The photo is looking south along the west side of Norfolk Street.

The *Simcoe Reformer*, Thursday, May 30, 1912, had the following to say about the May 24, Holiday Circus:

"Tis but a short week ago that the circus was here. Also 'twas but a short circus. It was a babes-in-the-wood parade with a Ringling Bros. admission price."

"There was a brass band and another one, a ticket wagon, a spiritless camel, one only lonely elephant, a clown donkey outfit, a snake and a snake charmer."

"What are circuses coming to? Where are circuses going to? — not Simcoe — not lately."

The opening of the Potts, Clarke Company, 12 Norfolk St. S., was given in the *British Canadian*, Wednesday, October 1, 1902:

"THE POTTS, CLARKE COMPANY"
"Opening of their new departmental store in Simcoe. For the past month, masons, carpenters, painters, decorators and other people have been working in the buildings lately occupied by G.T. Mitchell and H.W. Clarke and Company, preparing them for the occupancy by the Potts, Clarke Company."

Looking south from the Robinson Street corner. Murdoch's Dry Goods was located at 6-10 Norfolk Street South. Murdoch's placed the following advertisement in the Simcoe Reformer, *November 16, 1916: "Hats for Every Need of Every Smart Woman in Town. Clearing Prices on Thursday and Friday on velvet and plush winter millinery. Hats up to regular $4.00 choice $2.40; hats regular up to $6.50 choice $4.48.*

West side of Norfolk Street — circa 1959. Looking south along the west side of Norfolk Street from the Robinson Street corner. The buildings are the same but many of the tenants have changed. Murdoch's was taken over by the Henry R. Crabb Stores which later became Walker Stores. In the 1970's the building was taken over by Marks and Spencer. In April of 1978 a new tenant, Silvers, set up shop, carrying on the long line of drygoods stores in this one location.

The Checkered Store — circa 1880, south-west corner of Norfolk & Robinson Streets, from a painting by W.E. Cantelon

One of the earliest known stores in the Town of Simcoe stood on the south-west corner of Robinson and Norfolk Streets. It was built and operated by the Curtis family. How long it stood there, no one seems to know. It was known for thirty miles around as "The Checkered Store", a white and black block design of a painter, George Battersby, who came to Simcoe in 1836 and painted the Checkered Store before joining the host of 49ers in the gold rush to California. On his return, he became a local hotel keeper and the name Battersby is still familiar in Simcoe.

The Checkered Store was moved off the corner in 1893 and relocated on the south side of Water Street. It was purchased by the late R.E. Gunton who operated it as a carpenter shop for many years. It was replaced by the two-storey pressed brick building which still stands on the site and which was erected in 1893.

The following ad appeared in the *British Canadian*, Jan. 10, 1866:

"FRESH GROCERIES, CHECKERED STORE"
"50 chests extra fine fresh teas (crop of 1865), also new raisins, currants, candied peels, figs, prunes, lemons, almonds, filberts, fine English and American cheese, prime Labrador herrings in barrels and half-barrels, pickled haddock, mackerel in kits, Loch fine herring, fresh salmon in cans, potted meats, etc., with a large stock of choice family groceries."

"Just received and for sale cheap by J. Curtis, Simcoe, November 20, 1865."

1869. NEW SPRING GOODS. 1869.

H. W. Brethour & Co.,

WOULD beg to acquaint the public that the whole of their Spring Stock has arrived, and they would respectfully request an early inspection. Their Stock, which has been bought from the manufacturers direct, will be found to be one of the

Most Complete in Simcoe

And consists of the following

New and Fashionable Dress Goods!
BLACK AND COLORED

SILKS, POPLINS,

Berages, Muslins, Prints,

Cottons, Linens,

LACE CURTAINS, CURTAIN LACE, CURTAIN DAMASKS

Carpet in wool, 2 and 3 ply,

TAPESTRY, UNION AND HEMP!

FLOOR OIL CLOTH, &C. &C.

Also, a first-class lot of

Tweeds & Doeskins

H. W. BRETHOUR & CO.

J. B. BOOTH, Manager.
Simcoe, May 17, 1869.   ern5

On the west side of Norfolk Street, just past Robinson Street corner, were the firms of Austin, Werrett & Co., Hendry & Walsh and H.W. Brethour & Co.

The following newspaper articles give some information on these three firms. From the Port Dover *Maple Leaf*, June 20, 1890:

"We regret to announce that the old firm of Austin, Werrett & Potts, Simcoe, have been compelled to suspend payment on account of heavy purchases and inability to collect payments. As their assets are large, they will probably soon resume business. The firm has much sympathy in their financial trouble."

From the *Norfolk Reformer*, Mar. 12, 1868:
NEW STORE
"By reference to our advertising columns it will be seen that Messrs. H.W. Brethour Company will open on Wednesday next a new store in Simcoe, in conjunction with their establishment in Brantford. This firm have already received their Spring importations from Europe. The reputation which Messrs. H.W. Brethour and Company have enjoyed for selling first-class goods in Brantford at reasonable rates is a sufficient guarantee that their store in Simcoe will be in all respects worthy of the patronage of the public and we doubt not but that they will receive a liberal support at the hands of our readers. The two stores recently occupied by Messrs. L.G. and S.M. Sovereen have been made into one and are being fitted up with every regard to taste and convenience and we advise our readers to call and see the goods when opened. Mr. J.R. Booth is to remain here as Manager of the branch establishment."

Brethour and Company closed during the fall of 1870 and this property was taken over by A.J. Donly in September 1870.

On March 10th, 1870 the *Norfolk Reformer* reported:

"A new store will be opened in Simcoe in a few days by Messrs. Hendry and Walsh in the premises recently occupied by Mr. A.A. Merrill. The store is being refitted in preparation for the stock which will consist of a general assortment of drygoods, millinery in all its branches, etc. The new firm have our best wishes for success".

Austin, Werrett & Co., Hendry & Walsh and H.W. Brethour & Co. — circa 1870.
The Checkered Store can be seen on the far right.

The "Golden Horseshoe" business was owned by Charles Chadwick in 1880 at the site of 20 Norfolk Street (Pro Hardware). He was a merchant in groceries, china, crockery and glassware. A fire partially destroyed this building as seen in the following

The "Golden Horseshoe", west side of Norfolk Street — circa 1885

write-up from the *British Canadian*, April 20, 1887:

THE WORK OF AN INCENDIARY

"Last Wednesday night about eleven o'clock, flames were observed issuing from the door at the rear of the grocery and crockery store of Mr. Charles A. Chadwick in the centre of the block on the west side of Norfolk Street between Robinson and Peel Streets."

"The observers shouted ''Fire'' and a number of our townsmen who live in the vicinity and who had not retired, hastened to the store and found the whole west end of the room in flames and the building filled with smoke."

"With well-directed efforts the fire was soon put out. It was, however, a narrow escape as the flames had eaten through the ceiling and were commencing to spread under the floor in the second storey."

H. Carter's Shoe Store, 16 Norfolk St. S. is also seen here sometime before it became known as the Checkered Front Store.

Austin & Werrett were located at 14 Norfolk Street for many years.

West side Norfolk Street, just past Robinson Street corner — circa 1928

JUST ARRIVED,
AT
Austin, Werrett & Co.'s
The BEST and LARGEST lot of
CROCKERY
IN THE COUNTY.
Ironstone China
Tea sets,
Dinner sets,
Chamber sets,
China Tea and Breakfast sets,
Willow and C.. ware,
Stone Fruit Jars,
Stone Butter Crocks,
Stone churns
All kinds of GRANITE ware, by the piece or dozen.
Simcoe, May 29, 1867.   445-9

Henry R. Crabb had originally worked for Harvey Falls. About 1925 he took over the management of the Henry R. Crabb Store in Simcoe which later became known as Walker Stores. There were several stores, as such, throughout Southern Ontario.

An advertisement in the *Simcoe Reformer*, August 26, 1926 boasted:

"Our first Birthday Sale will close on Saturday, August 28th, at 10 p.m. Many thrifty shoppers have visited our store during the great selling event and have found the goods they required and at very moderate prices for reliable merchandise. We are placing new lines at special prices for the last two days of this sale."

"3 lb. large comforter bats 72 x 90 size, white and fluffy, each 95¢ —

Ladies' and Misses' dresses, 47 only, new pirouette twill, wool, faille, khassia flannel, etc. Not an old one in the lot, no two the same style. Our special price . . . $7.95"

THE HENRY R. CRABB STORES,
   Your Favourite Shopping Centre;
   PAY CASH AND BUY FOR LESS

The exceptionally fine photograph on the opposite page of the west side of Norfolk Street, shows a group of horses and wagons ready to leave on a Sunday School picnic, probably for Fisher's Glen or Port Dover. The photographer was standing approximately in front of the present Bank of Montreal looking north along the west side of Norfolk Street. Notice the J. Austin Drug Company, 26 Norfolk Street South; Madden Bros. Souvenirs, Stoves and Ranges, 24 Norfolk Street South; Carter's Checkered Front Store, 16 Norfolk Street South, and in the far background the H.S. Falls Company which was then located where the present Woolworth Store stands.

This rare photo was given to the author by long-time friend and sport's enthusiast, the late John Leask.

The following article and advertisement appeared in the *British Canadian*:
MAY 6, 1896 — "On Monday morning a team of horses belonging to a farmer named Fairchild became frightened at a piece of loose paper on the street while standing in front of Austin's Drug Store and dashed down the street at breakneck speed. They were pluckily caught by Mr. Del Woolley near Allen's corner (corner of Peel and Norfolk) without doing any damage. The practise of throwing paper on the street is a bad one and any person doing so should be punished."
JUNE 24, 1891 — "Messrs. Palmerton & Madden are having plans and specifications prepared for the new block they propose erecting on Norfolk Street. It will be the King of business places in Simcoe."

The previous building at this location had partially burned out April 13, 1887.

This interior photo on this page gives one an idea of the intricate design of the early stoves and ranges carried by this store at the turn of the century. An advertisement in the *Simcoe Reformer*, November 16, 1916 claims:
"Easily rocked are the three-bar grates which smash up clinkers easily and last longer because each grate is three-sided."
"McCLARY'S PANDORA RANGE"
"The man who designed the Pandora knew his job. I know that, and that is why it carries my guarantee as well as the maker's."
Sold by J.H. Madden.

Interior of Palmerton & Madden Store, 24 Norfolk Street south — circa 1900

Downtown Simcoe, west side of Norfolk Street — circa 1898

Carter's Checkered Front Shoe Store — circa 1910

A popular downtown landmark for years was Carter's Shoe Store on the west side of Norfolk Street South. The following ad appeared in the *Simcoe Reformer*, September 7, 1906: "Checkered Front Shoe Store now ready for Fall Trade. We are agents for the Winner Shoes for infants, girls, misses, youths and boys. We carry a full line of the above make consisting of patents, box and velour calf, dongolas, pebbles, etc. We will stand back of every pair. The price will meet with your approval. We buy direct from the factory. We know what is in these shoes. Call and we will tell you. The Checkered Front Shoe Store in Simcoe. We have no connection with any other store. If you want the best, see us."

This store was located on the west side of Norfolk Street South, No. 16. The store was started in 1852 by Henry Carter, and continued by his sons Ernest E. and Harry A. This business continued until 1951 giving a business span of 99 years. This was the oldest shoe store in Canada under the same family. It nearly burned in 1903 as we learn from a news item in the *British Canadian*, May 6, 1903: "The fire alarm rang at noon on Thursday caused by a furiously burning chimney in the Carter Shoe Store. No damage was done."

In the photograph is Fred Purcel, a member of the staff, who later became the proprietor of the Lyric Theatre.

This photo was taken from about the corner of Norfolk and Sydenham Streets looking south-west, on the occasion of the visit of Prince Arthur and Sir John Young, the Governor-General of Canada, September 28, 1869.

The following appeared in The Simcoe Reformer's 100th Anniversary Edition, September 29, 1958:
"On September 28th, 1869, His Royal Highness, Prince Arthur and Sir John Young, the Governor General of Canada, visited Simcoe."

"September 28th will long be remembered as a red-letter day in the history of the inhabitants of this county."

"Three evergreen arches were formed on Norfolk Street, the first one being placed near the corner of Norfolk and Sydenham Streets, the second at the corner of Norfolk and Argyle Streets and the third at the corner of Norfolk and Peel Streets. They were all beautifully decorated with evergreens, wreaths and flowers and all bore suitable inscriptions, tribute to the visiting dignitaries. Beside the arches a large number of evergreens were stretched across the streets, interspersed with red, white and blue."

"The buildings, too, were handsomely decorated; flags were flying and the whole scene was picturesque in the extreme. At the entrance to the town, the people of Wellington had erected a fine arch of evergreens augmented with a wreath of Maple leaves and flowers and the word "Welcome" in red letters."

Hayes & Livingstone's "Drug Emporium" at 32-36 Norfolk Street South sold everything from stationary, wallpaper to fancy goods and, of course, Patent Medicines.

Next door at No. 38, Jas. Anderson Shoe Store advertised in the Norfolk Reformer, December 22, 1870:
"James Anderson of the Montreal Boot and Shoe Store has on hand a large stock of ladies' and gents' and children's boots and shoes."

Norfolk Street South — September 28, 1869

Norfolk Street South — circa 1910, looking north along the west side of Norfolk Street from about the Sydenham Street intersection. At that time Brook Clothing Company occupied 36 Norfolk St. S.; Baillie Book Store, books & novelties, No. 32; Counter's Jewellery, watches, locksmith, No. 28; J. Austin & Company, drugs & wallpapers, No. 26; Madden Bros., stoves and ranges, No. 22.

Counter's Jewellery began in 1856 in the Empire Block. Later they had a store in the Norfolk House Block and then in 1874 moved to its last site at 28 Norfolk St. S.

The Brook Clothing Company advertised in the British Canadian, June 24, 1896: "Special sale, children's clothing. Big bargains. See our window display for next 10 days but do not stay outside. Come in and examine them and you will be convinced that we are offering the best obtainable goods for the money. Suits for $1.48, $1.98, $2.20, $2.25 and upwards."

Window display advertising "Quaker Oats" in the George H. Widner store, 24 Norfolk St. S. — circa 1905. Among the specials of the day were: 5 lb. bag oatmeal, 25¢; Navel Oranges, 30¢ per dozen. The premises were later occupied by R.G. Holmes & Anderson, Pro Hardware.

Looking north along Norfolk Street, this photograph was taken by G.R. Perry on April 7, 1886, just after the great snowstorm that plugged the streets and cut Simcoe off from the surrounding area. C. C. Jackson, operated the "Red Star Grocery" at the corner of Peel and Norfolk. Next door at No. 44, we see the Oscar Hendry Store, and at No. 42, G. R. Perry, photographer.

The Oscar Hendry Store advertised their goods in the Port Dover *Independent*, June 28, 1878: "Ten Thousand Dollars" worth of seasonal drygoods and millinery, in all the latest styles and best makes; goods that had been purchased upon the most favourable terms. New and fresh; (no old stock); and best of all the lowest prices. Hundreds of ladies' trimmed hats and bonnets, the very newest . . . . 75¢ up. At the Golden Bee Hive, Simcoe, Oscar Hendry."

Once more Simcoe was struck by fire, as we learn from this report in the *British Canadian*, Wednesday, December 7, 1892:

"BURNING OF PERRY'S BLOCK"

"Last Saturday morning about four o'clock the town was aroused by the fire alarm when it was discovered that the back portion of the brick block owned and occupied by Mr. George R. Perry on Norfolk Street opposite the Norfolk House, was a mass of flames. The fire, fanned by the strong west wind, readily swept through the building rendering it impossible to save any of its contents consisting of art and photographic gallery, and stock of fancy goods. The goods of Mr. Falls on the north were more or less damaged while the stock of Mr. Hendry was almost entirely ruined by the water and smoke. The burned block was owned by Mr. Perry who was particularly unfortunate as the whole of his valuable stock of negatives, the accumulation of twenty years, was destroyed together with his books."

The "Great Snowstorm", April 7, 1886

West side of Norfolk Street, April 7, 1886; looking north from about the Syndenham Street intersection.

Looking north from the Sydenham Street intersection, this photo shows the rest of "Perry's Block".

In the foreground can be seen the Jas. Anderson Shoe Store (38 Norfolk St. S.) and towards the middle of the block the boot sign for H. Carter's Shoe Store (16 Norfolk St. S.).

The following news item appeared in the *British Canadian*, Wednesday, March 9, 1892:

"The Brick block in which Mr. Anderson's Shoe Store is situated had a narrow escape from destruction by fire on Thursday night. On Friday morning on opening the doors of the shop, the place was found full of smoke and the floor on fire near the flue in the chimney."

The corner store, 48 Norfolk Street South, and the adjacent building, 44 Norfolk Street South, to the north, have a long history of tenants.

Reportedly built by Owen H. Falls in 1834, the corner building was gutted by fire in January of 1892. Mr. Falls operated a grocery store here for some years and then leased it to John Logan. James Perry and Captain David Swinton succeeded Logan and then Mr. Perry carried on for some time.

He was succeeded by McCosh and Menzie. Fred Lansdill was for some time afterwards the owner of the business. Then came Byrne and Augustine, followed by Edmund Birk who called the business "The Red Star Grocery". George Allan came next and then C. C. Jackson (1886); then James Moe who was succeeded by J. C. Watson. Mr. Watson was the proprietor of the grocery at the time of the 1892 fire. In the offices upstairs at the time, Dr. C. Fitton had his dental surgery. Also on the second floor were Bruce Jackson, a lawyer, and Charles E. Barber, another lawyer.

A. E. Christmas was also owner of the grocery business for some time and in 1903 Walter S. McCall had a grocery business there.

At the time Martin Bros. rented the store, a man named Riley was proprietor. Martin Bros. started in 1906 and in December of 1971 R. J. "Bob" Castles continued as proprietor of this long established business.

The companion store to the north has not had nearly as long a list of proprietors. Mr. Falls was also the owner of this store and for some years his son William Falls and Alexander Tocher had an establishment within its walls, probably men's furnishings or drygoods. Following them was Allan H. Walsh who was senior partner for awhile with Oscar Hendry as junior partner. Mr. Hendry then became sole owner of the drygoods business and called his store "The Golden Bee Hive". Early in the century, Fred R. Pursel had a shoestore there and he gave way to Perry Weston who conducted a pool room there before he became associated with Arthur C. Lea.

George P. Gettas was, for years, owner of the confectionery and restaurant enterprise, following a former Mayor of Simcoe, David R. Austin who had a furniture emporium there. After Mr. Gettas, George Bukydes carried on The Tops Restaurant in the same location. Then came Sam Berger and Son, Eaton's Order Office, and in August of 1962, George Snyder Shoes.

The following article appeared in the *British Canadian* May 9, 1892:

FIRE IN SIMCOE

"On Sunday night, about half-past eleven, fire broke out in the centre of the building on the corner of Norfolk and Peel Streets owned by Mr. O. H. Falls and occupied by Mr. J. C. Watson, grocer, and Mr. C. H. Fitton, dentist. The fire, when first seen, had made such headway that only a few dollars worth of the contents of the grocery could be saved, while it was impossible to enter the dental rooms above."

"The adjoining store also owned by Mr. Falls, but occupied by Mr. Oscar Hendry who carried a heavy stock of drygoods, was in jeopardy and the firemen found it necessary to pour a large quantity of water into the upper portion of it to keep it from burning."

An advertisement in the *Simcoe Reformer*, Nov. 16, 1916, placed by Martin Bros. stated:

"YE OLD FIRME . . . THE LAST WORD."
"The beautiful tone and tonal volume, the handsome external appearance, the great simplicity in operating, the patented weatherproof aluminum action, the permanency of tone and construction, makes the Heintzman & Company Player Piano the last word in player piano construction."

"It is made by expert and experienced Canadian workmen in a Canadian factory by a Canadian firm. It is built to last a lifetime and can easily be played by anyone old or young without the operator knowing a note of music. Any class of music can be rendered on this wonderful instrument and most beautiful effects obtained."

Ritchie, Ford & Co., south-west corner of Norfolk & Peel Streets — circa 1865

The Ritchie, Ford and Company operated the Simcoe Mills for many years at the foot of Water Street. They also ran a general store in the early 1850's at the south-east corner of Water and Norfolk Streets. However, this building was apparently too small and they moved to the south-west corner of Norfolk & Peel Streets in 1859. The old building became a warehouse which burned in 1870. The *Norfolk Reformer*, March 10, 1870 reported: "The Ritchie, Ford and Company Warehouse on the corner of Norfolk and Water Streets was destroyed by fire. The Post Office, a few feet south, had a narrow escape."

"As usual, one engine was taken to the fire by some person but it could not be got to work, no one knowing how to manage it, and after a couple of vain attempts to get it to throw water it was allowed to remain idle. So much for the efficiency of our fire department."

The account goes on to say that two kegs of powder exploded during the fire.

The firm announced their move to the new premises in the *Norfolk Messenger*, March, 29, 1859 with this notice: "The subscribers, thankful for the liberal support afforded them for many years past, beg to acquaint their friends and the public that they have removed to the handsome new premises at the corner of Norfolk and Peel Streets where they will offer the extensive assortment of drygoods, groceries and hardware at very reduced prices. Cash paid for wheat, rye, corn and barley."

On August 28, 1874, the same day that "Lord Dufferin", the Governor-General of Canada, visited Simcoe, the above store was destroyed by fire. The *Simcoe*

Reformer reported the fire in the September 3 edition as follows:

"On Thursday night last, a short time after the people of the town had wended their way home from visiting the court house square, witnessing the presentation of some of our eminent citizens to their Excellencies, the Governor-General and Countess of Dufferin, they were startled to hear the cry of 'Fire'."

"Some thought at first that the alarm was raised for the purpose of creating a sensation but in a very short time it proved only too true. On arriving at the scene of the conflagration we found that the inside of Mr. Gallagher's boot and shoe store was on fire."

"The flames soon spread south to Mr. Thos. Townley's tailoring establishment and house and the building, being of wood, was soon reduced to ashes."

"The next building north was the large brick store on the corner of Peel and Norfolk Streets, owned by Dr. Wilson and occupied as a dry goods and grocery store by Messrs. N. C. Ford and Company."

"We feel bound to say that N. C. Ford's warehouse should have been saved. There is blame to be attached somewhere. We have witnessed several fires in Simcoe but we fail to call to mind a more unmanageable crowd than the one we saw at the fire on Thursday night. We hope that pains will be taken to enforce better discipline in the future. Numbers of people stood and looked on with their hands in their pockets or pipe in their mouth, or something in their eye and would not lend a helping hand to form a line for the purpose of passing water to the engine."

Canadian Bank of Commerce, south-west corner of Norfolk & Peel Streets — circa 1890

Following the great fire of August 28, 1874, which destroyed the building occupied by Ritchie, Ford & Company, the owner, Dr. John Wilson, erected this large 7-store brick block. One of the main tenants until 1923 was the Canadian Bank of Commerce which occupied the corner location. Other information about tenants is found in these notices from various issues of the *British Canadian*.

APRIL 27, 1887 — "We understand Z. Landon Esq. has purchased from the Federal Bank that valuable property in this town known as Dr. Wilson's Block which is situated on the south side of Peel Street and extends from Norfolk to Brock Street." (Brock Street is now Kent Street.)

SEPTEMBER 19, 1888 — "Mr. Joseph Carter has opened his Boot & Shoe Store in the Chadwick Block nearly opposite the Post Office on Peel Street. Give him a call at his new premises."

NOVEMBER 28, 1888 — "Messrs. Bray and Company have removed their cabinet warerooms from the old stand at Mr. James Bray's to 999 in Dr. Wilson's Block, Peel St. They have received a very heavy stock from the best manufacturers in the Dominion and have now one of the largest and most complete assortments to be found in any establishment in the Province. The store is packed full and parties in want of furniture cannot fail to be suited. There is no necessity for going to the cities to buy furniture."

"Persons living on the line of the South Norfolk Railway making purchases at the 999 Peel Street of $25.00 and over and showing their ticket, will be allowed the cost of their ticket and a dinner ticket, at the 999 Peel Street. Parties on the line of Railway showing their ticket and buying goods to the amount of $5.00 will receive a ticket for hotel dinner free, at the 999 Peel Street."

AUGUST 20, 1890 — "Messrs. Mallory have opened a Billiard Parlour in the Doctor Wilson Block in the shop lately occupied by James W. Bray. It is furnished with three modern tables."

Looking north on Norfolk Street from Peel Street — circa 1915

Downtown — East side of Norfolk Street

The above photo was taken by John Rutherford — circa 1900, from the roof of the Bank of Commerce Building (at that time on the south-west corner of Peel and Norfolk Streets), looking north along the east side of Norfolk Street. Notice the trees in the far background starting at the north-east corner of Argyle and Norfolk Streets. This was all part of the Campbell Estate at that time. The Norfolk Hotel, at the south-east corner of Norfolk and Sydenham Streets, did not have the elaborate front verandah which was added later. As we see in the photo on the right, it greatly enhanced its appearance. On the north-east corner of Sydenham and Norfolk Streets can be seen the Anderson Hardware sign dating back to 1886. Next is the Molson's Bank which took over the whole of the Groff Block in 1908.

On the north-east corner of Norfolk and Argyle Streets can be seen the Falls Department Store which was completed in 1912.

Little can be seen on the west side of Norfolk Street except for a few signs, namely: The Hub Clothing Store, Moore Photography Studio at No. 34 Norfolk Street and Brook Clothing Store.

Horse drawn sleigh-bus which was used for delivering passengers to and from the Norfolk Hotel and the train station — circa 1912

The Norfolk Hotel

The original Norfolk Hotel was destroyed by fire on March 18, 1863, and plans were immediately made to rebuild. The *Norfolk Reformer* of August 10, 1865, contained the following encomium about the re-opening:
"Opening of the Norfolk House. This splendid hotel was opened for the reception of guests on Monday last. It has been furnished in the very best style by the lessee, Mr. George Battersby, and cannot be surpassed for comfort and convenience by any hotel in western Canada. The Band favoured Mr. Battersby with a serenade on Monday evening in honor of the opening of the house. We bespeak for the Norfolk patronage which the enterprise fully merits."

The Opera House in the Norfolk Hotel was a very popular place of entertainment for some forty-four years until it was destroyed by fire on Nov. 1, 1909. Travelling Minstrel Shows, Band Concerts, Local Theatre groups, High School plays, were all performed there.

The *British Canadian* of May 1, 1895, contained an ad about a special performance of the Paris Gaiety Girls. However, the following paper, May 8, 1895, had this to say about their show: "The Paris Gaiety Girls secured a very poor house on Wednesday night. The audience was composed principally of boys who would have been better off under the parental roof. The show was a poor affair and the bald-headed jokes were old enough to be buried. The party left town under a cloud."

Later, from the *British Canadian*, June 19, 1895, we read: "Sam Pickett, Manager of the Paris Gaiety Girl's Company, found guilty of conducting an immoral show, was on Saturday sentenced by Judge Ermatinger to a month in jail. Pickett has already been in jail a month, so that he will have served a two month sentence in effect."

Fire struck the Hotel on November 1, 1909. The *Simcoe Reformer* reported in the Nov. 4, 1909 edition: "Fire again visits Simcoe. One of the most substantial blocks falls a victim of flames, Opera House Block destroyed; Norfolk House badly damaged."

"At a few minutes past three a.m., Monday morning, policeman Sharpe discovered smoke issuing from the front of the Dreamland Theatorium, the property of Mr. Thomas Hurley situated in the south portion of the Opera House Block."

Because of the firewalls between the Opera House and the Hotel, the Hotel was partially saved. The Opera House, Mr. Gamble's Cigar Store and Billiard Room were completely destroyed. The upper two stores of the Norfolk House were badly gutted.

The fire was thought to have started in the back of the Dreamland Theatre.

The fire completely wiped out the Opera House, the roof and the third floor of the Norfolk Hotel. However, the rest of the building was saved and, shortly after the fire, repairs were underway to modernize the whole structure. The Opera House was eliminated in the restoration.

After the fire — November 2, 1909

The Opera House in the Norfolk Hotel. This photo, by E. S. B. Moore, was taken in the Opera House around 1905. The man in the middle is probably J. D. Christie, the first Principal of Simcoe High School.

Norfolk Hotel — circa 1915

Norfolk House,
SIMCOE.

THIS splendid hotel, which has been furnished in a very superior style, is now open to the public. The larders will always be supplied with the choicest provisions, and the best of liquors will be kept constantly on hand.

Good stabling and attentive hostlers in attendance.

Terms reasonable.

GEO. BATTERSBY,
Proprietor.

351

Simcoe, Aug. 7, 1865.

The scene on the right, photographed on February 20, 1957, shows the remains of the Norfolk Hotel following the fire of February 19, 1957. The Simcoe Reformer, *February 20, 1957 reported:*
"Norfolk Hotel is destroyed by Fire. Loss estimated at $250,000.00 in ruinous all-night blaze. Firemen put up great battle."
"The Norfolk Hotel stands in smoking ruins this morning devasted by the biggest fire here since Falls' Department Store burned in 1937. A spectacular blaze defied firemen for six hours and then took another four hours to subside, completely burned out the hotel and threatened to spread to adjacent buildings before firemen from six departments brought it under control."
In the background can be seen the Norfolk Glass and Mirror at 65 Norfolk Street South. The King Block adjacent to the south end of the hotel, was destroyed by fire on May 20, 1977.

King's Garage & Meat Market — circa 1925

The King Building at 55-61 Norfolk St. S. was erected in 1905 by Henry H. Hoffmann. The building, at the head of Peel Street, has seen many changes. It was originally used for a furniture business and an undertaking establishment. In 1912, Hoffmann sold to Mr. E. F. Best who carried on the same business until 1919 when ill health forced him to retire. In that year the building was bought by Samuel L. King who at that time was operating a garage business on Colborne Street. Mr. King carried on his garage business until 1925 when he opened up a butcher shop in one part of the building and a second-hand furniture store and auction rooms in the other part. In 1926 the building was divided into three sections, the north being used as offices, the centre as a clothing store and the south being occupied by Johnson Plumbing which later became Johnson Bros.

After the Second World War, the Unemployment Commission vacated the south section of the building and it then became Porter's Stationery. About the same time the north section was rented to Carl High Electric and when they vacated in 1949, Western Tire occupied the store for a year. In 1951 Morrison Appliances Limited moved into the north section. When Porter's Stationery moved to Norfolk Street North, Mr. Morrison also took over the south part for a Television Lounge and Used Appliances outlet.

The building was renovated in 1957 and changed into two sections, King's and Morrison's, and remained that way until the destructive fire of May 20th, 1977.

1920 Chevrolets in front of Samuel L. King's Garage.

Best's Furniture Store — circa 1916

Looking south along the east side of Norfolk Street, from Peel Street — circa 1905. This is one of the few early photographs showing the Historic Empire Block built north of Water Street. This was probably a May 24 or July 1 celebration as either days would usually feature various types of running races. In the centre background can be seen C. E. Mitchell, Agent for Cockshutt Plow Company, located at 65 Norfolk Street.

The E. F. Best Furniture Store, located at 55-61 Norfolk Street South placed this advertisement in the *Simcoe Reformer*, November 16, 1916:

"Auction Sale, Unconditional Surrender to the Public of the E. F. Best Furniture & Rug Stock. A $25,000 stock of high-grade furniture and house furnishings. Commencing Saturday, November 18, at 2:30 and 7:30 p.m."

"The most sweeping and far-reaching sale in the history of Simcoe. This splendid stock, acknowledged the finest in this part of Canada under the hammer. Do you wonder why we do it? We are heavily overstocked and must reduce, so come and help yourself at auction and special sale. We want the cash."

"We will pay your railway fare on any purchase of $25.00 from any point within 25 miles."

Looking north on Norfolk Street from Peel Street — circa 1945

One of the more modern changes in downtown Simcoe was the establishment of by-laws forbidding the use of overhanging signs in front of store buildings. The neon signs so prevalent in this photo became one of the accepted ways of advertising in the 30's and 40's before the by-laws.

Notice the Union Jack flying over the Bank of Montreal. The old Capital Theatre building (9 Norfolk Street South) fell victim to the Television Syndrome of the 50's.

On the left (west side of Norfolk Street) notice the large neon sign on the front of Gettas' Restaurant.

Gettas' Restaurant dated back to the early 1920's. It was for years a very popular eating establishment and became one of the favorite places for High School Students to spend their free time after school. At the front of the restaurant glass counters would always be filled with their delicious "home-made" candies and chocolates. Its lucky for today's diet-conscious Simconians, that prices have changed. Advertising in the Simcoe Reformer, June 15, 1922, Gettas' offered the "Saturday Specials" — Peppermint Wafers, 29¢ per lb.; French Nuggat, 34¢ per lb. and Toasted Marshmallow, 29¢ per lb.

Souvenir Postcard, Gettas' Restaurant, 44 Norfolk Street South — circa 1940

This is the best known photo taken by G. R. Perry of the 'Great Snow Storm' of April 6 and 7, 1886, looking north along the east side of Norfolk Street from the Sydenham Street corner.

The following news article appeared in the *British Canadian* on March 11, 1885:

"FIRE: A CLOSE CALL"

"On Thursday evening last, the Federal Bank Block, the property of Henry Groff Esq., and in which are situated the Federal Bank, Mr. Hearst's Drygoods Store, Mr. Dobson's Book Store and Telegraph Office, and Mr. Anderson's Hardware Store on the ground floor, and the printing office of The Norfolk Reformer in the upper storey, had a narrow escape from destruction by fire."

"The destruction of the block would have been a serious loss to Mr. Groff and a disaster to the town and it is very creditable to the townspeople and the brigade who worked so manfully that it was saved from destruction."

In 1881 Wallace Anderson purchased the hardware establishment of James Dunlop on the corner of Sydenham and Norfolk Streets. Mr. Anderson was five years of age, when he had come to Simcoe with his father, James Anderson, veteran shoe merchant, in 1885. He became an apprentice in the hardware establishment of Thomas Hepplewhite on the south-east corner of Norfolk and Argyle Streets, which later became the H. F. Prelipp Hardware Store. Three generations of Andersons carried on business here until it was destroyed by fire on August 19th, 1965.

The Federal Bank which was closed in 1888 was located in the north end of this building block.

Looking south-east on Norfolk Street from Robinson Street — circa 1896

Notice on the east side of Norfolk Street, the Bank of Hamilton Building, No. 23 (present location of the Bank of Montreal). The Norfolk Hotel at that time had a covered entry at the front door.

Terry & Culver Dry Goods, located at about No. 10 Norfolk Street South, advertised June 24, 1896 in the *British Canadian*: "Are you fond of Money? Do you save Money? Do you know how to do it?"

"If you want to know, visit our clothing department. We are making a specialty of clothing, and nowhere else in Simcoe are there such bargains as we can show you. We have the celebrated blue serge suits which are selling so readily at $2.90 in almost every store in Simcoe — our price $2.48."
Signed: Terry and Culver
EGGS WANTED.

No. 21 Norfolk Street South — circa 1867. In the archives of the Eva Brook Donly Museum an article was found describing Simcoe in 1867. The following is an excerpt from that article: "We now return to Norfolk Street and go south. Where C. E. Boyd's storehouse stood was a frame building occupied by John Sullivan's Shoe Shop, Harris' Shoe Store, Mrs. Waters' Bakery, John Greg's Saloon and Oyster Parlour, and Asa A. Purcel's Livery and Stage Stables where the Bank of Montreal now stands. This row of buildings all burned the same night. In the rear of the livery stable there stood a large frame building used as a drill hall and armouries with entrance on Norfolk Street."

The Bank of Hamilton — circa 1890

The Bank of Hamilton was one of the Town's older banking institutions. It was first opened in the north half of the building now occupied by the Bank of Montreal at 23 Norfolk Street South. To the south of the Bank of Hamilton building were the offices of the Simcoe Reformer at that time.

In 1898 the Bank of Hamilton moved to the south-east corner of Norfolk and Argyle Streets. On May 7th, 1898 Molson's Bank took over the vacated premises at 21 Norfolk Street South and modernized the north half only of the building. By 1908 they had purchased the whole of the 'Groff' Block and remodelled the whole building into their banking offices. In 1937 the building was refaced with more modern brick material.

Advertising in the *Simcoe Reformer*, November 16, 1916, Molson's Bank stated:

"Incorporated 1855. The Molson's Bank, Capital & Reserve $8,800,000, 96 Branches in Canada. A general banking business transacted. Circular letters of credit, Bank Money Orders, Savings Bank Department. Interest allowed at highest current rate."

Molson's Bank — circa 1910

Above: South-east corner Norfolk & Argyle Streets — circa 1885. The photograph on the left, taken circa 1905, shows the new Bank of Hamilton building. The poster in front of the bank is advertising a play called "The Bonnie Brier Bush", at the Opera House in the Norfolk Hotel, January 14.

The building at 5 Norfolk Street South where the Bank of Commerce is now situated, was previously occupied by Prelipp-Schott Hardware (and W. W. Walsh & Son Furniture). It was built many years ago by Simcoe's first Postmaster Duncan Campbell. T. Hebblewhite had a hardware store business here opened in October, 1864. Gordon & Ellis date back to at least 1871. Above the store on the second floor, the old British Canadian, which was taken over in August of 1926 by the Simcoe Reformer, was published. Mr. Ellis conducted the hardware store himself for some years after Mr. Gordon's death. Through the door off Argyle Street were the law offices of Tisdale and Livingstone.

The site was purchased by the Bank of Hamilton in 1898. They tore down the old two-storey brick building and half of the brick wall that enclosed the storage yard of the hardware business. The new building was large enough to contain the bank in the corner location and the hardware store immediately south. However, the front wall to the storage yard now had a lopsided or tilted appearance rather than the pleasing peaked lines of before.

Some time later, the late Charles E. Boyd became the owner occupying it successfully until 1921 when William Davidson purchased the business. He conducted it for about two years, selling to H. F. Prelipp who carried on the business for more than 30 years. In 1956, Mr. Prelipp retired and sold out to Mr. Donald Schott.

The corner location was sold in 1962 to the Bank of Commerce by W. W. Walsh & Son who had been in business in that location for 44 years dating back to 1918.

The construction of the Bank of Hamilton building is noted in the *British Canadian*, April 6, 1898:

"The contract for the erection of the Bank of Hamilton block on the corner of Norfolk and Argyle Streets was awarded to Mr. John Montgomery of this town, who erected the High School building, the Methodist Church and the Melbourne House. The demolition of the old building commenced on Monday morning. The building torn down had been erected in 1843 by the late D. Campbell and was the first work done in Simcoe by the late W. L. Smith."

Looking north on Norfolk Street from Sydenham Street — circa 1915. Notice the "Boots and Shoes" store of W. A. Hardie at 15 Norfolk Street South and The Simcoe Produce Company at 17 Norfolk Street South.

On Friday, January 24, 1908, the Simcoe Firemen tested the new waterworks system which was completed in 1907. Notice the stone fence running north along Norfolk Street. The H. S. Falls Company at this time was located in the Battersby Hotel Block (now Woolworth's location). The *Simcoe Reformer*, January 30, 1908, tells how the streams of water were effective to a height of 30 feet above the flagstaff on Falls Store.

Norfolk Theatre, Norfolk Street North — circa 1964

The Norfolk Theatre was located on the west side of Norfolk Street, about half-way between Robinson and Young Streets. This was a classy downtown theatre during the 40s, and 50s.

After the close of this theatre, around 1961, it was used by the Simcoe Little Theatre for their regular plays and by the Lion's Club for their Annual Minstrel Shows. Other uses were found for the auditorium as seen on the marquee above.

Simpsons-Sears, Fernlea Flowers and Ryerse Flowers were some of the several tenants who used the two retail store outlets over the years.

The building was torn down in 1965 to make way for an enlargement to Woolworth's Store.

Lynnwood Avenue, Duncan Campbell Home — circa 1907

The Duncan Campbell House

The Duncan Campbell house was built in 1852. The area comprising the Campbell estate ran from the corner of Norfolk and Argyle Streets along Norfolk to the Lynn River and east along Argyle to the river. A stone wall was built along the front of the property on Norfolk Street to the corner of the present Lynnwood Park.

Duncan Campbell died in 1892; the property passed to his son J. Lorne Campbell, Mayor of Simcoe, 1891-92. Lorne Campbell was thrice President of the Toronto Stock Exchange. He apparently went bankrupt around 1905 or 1906 and the Campbell estate was eventually broken up. For a few years this house was used as a private hospital by a Doctor Bennetto. It was purchased by Francis Reid in 1912. The Reid family however did not move into the house until about 1920. During the First World War, Mr. Reid turned the house over to the I.O.D.E. for their workrooms and their Belgium Relief parcel-packaging.

The above photo was taken from Lynnwood Avenue north of the dwelling, looking south. Lynnwood Avenue appears to have been started by the time the picture was taken indicating a date around 1907. Notice the servants' quarters, stables and water tower at the rear of the main house.

The *British Canadian* reported on September 2, 1891: "Mr. Campbell has had a splendid system of waterworks placed in his residence at Lynnwood. The hydraulic works and mains were put in by Mr. S. Sebring and the plumbing was done by Messrs. Palmerton & Madden. The water is brought from an excellent spring on the east side of the pond through which the pipes pass and is conveyed throughout the dwelling, outhouses and stable and hydrants are placed in different parts of the grounds giving a system that is probably not equalled in any private grounds in the Province."

In 1907 the Lynnwood Survey was laid out, and an arena was built that year by Charles Brookfield.

Duncan Campbell House and Brookfield Arena — circa 1908

The following articles from the *British Canadian* give some idea of the use and condition of Lynnwood during the war years.

MARCH 10, 1915 — "Thursday's shipment to Belgium weighed 59,000 pounds. The twelfth car shipped to Belgium from Norfolk County, under the auspices of the County Patriotic Aid Committee, got away as per the time table. The contributions were received at Lynnwood Headquarters."

MAY 3, 1916 — "Old Lynnwood occupied! The Daughters of The Empire have removed their headquarters to Lynnwood. If the presence of the centre of activity for the manufacture, collection and shipment of supplies to the camp or the trenches, effects a stoppage of the wanton destruction this grand old building has received during the past months, the occupation will be a blessing. Strange as it may seem, even adults have done part of the window smashing here, along with children of very respectable citizens."

These exceptionally fine interior views of Lynnwood were taken by E. S. B. Moore. It is believed that they were taken for Mr. Reid just after the home had been redecorated following the First World War and just after the Reid family had moved into the home.

In 1973 Lynnwood was designated a National Historic Site, and by December 4, 1974, the building had been restored to its original state and was officially opened as The Lynnwood Arts Centre.

The photo, top left, was taken from the front entrance, looking east towards the staircase leading to the second floor.

Top right: Taken from the south-east corner of the large north room this photo shows the two doors on the north wall which were once connected to the verandah along the north side of the house. These doors have since been closed in. Beyond the right door in the background can barely be seen the framework for one of the homes being constructed on the west side of Lynnwood Avenue. The survey on that street was laid out in 1907 and many of the homes were built by 1925.

Bottom left: The north room from the north-west corner looking south-east. Along the south wall of the room can be seen two of the many fireplaces that enhance this fine old home. In the restoration program of 1973-74, these fireplaces were preserved.

Bottom right: This is probably the upstairs back bedroom of the main part of the original house, looking west, the window being on the north wall. The two fireplaces once in the upper two north bedrooms, have been boxed in and the wall between these two rooms removed.

The Brookfield Arena

The Lynnwood survey was laid out in 1907 and the arena was built that year by Charles Brookfield on the east side of Lynnwood about half-way between Argyle Street and Lynnwood Park.

Notice the trees on the hills behind the arena and on the east side of the Lynn River. The men working are the crew of builder Charles Brookfield.

The Brookfield Arena was completed in December of 1907. Three years later in 1910 it was destroyed by fire.

The *Simcoe Reformer* Thursday January 16, 1908, said: "Many Skaters — Few in Costume — at the Opening Carnival at Lynnwood Rink. There was a fair attendance of spectators and a crowd of skaters at the carnival on Wednesday evening, but comparatively few in costume, the small fry being barred".

Brookfield Arena — circa 1908

The Mason Arena

The Mason Arena under construction — circa 1911

The new Mason Arena shortly after completion — circa 1912

The Mason Arena was built in 1911 by George Mason at a cost of $16,000. It was 76 feet by 196 feet and had a spectator capacity of 1,200. It was built on the east side of Lynnwood Avenue on the same site as the Brookfield Arena which had burned in 1910. In 1913 three sections of the roof collapsed but they were soon repaired.

Simcoe was always a hot-bed of hockey and many keen games were played in this arena. The season of 1937-38 saw the largest crowd — more than 1,500 when the Reformer Cubs went to the O.H.A. Junior Semi-Finals.

It was New Year's Day, Jan. 1, 1945, about 1:00 p.m. — Manager Stanley Cross had locked the arena doors following hockey practice which finished about noon. Many Simcoe children had already left their homes for an afternoon of skating — the doors would be open again at 2:00 pm. Suddenly without any warning the roof and walls of the arena crashed to the ice surface below. The Mason Arena was completely destroyed.

Cause of the collapse was attributed to the heavy snow which had been lying on the metal roof for some time. Had the collapse occurred one hour later between 2:00 and 3:00, children would have been skating on the ice surface, most of them without a doubt would have been killed or badly injured and so a tragedy of enormous proportions was missed by only an hour.

In the 1850's work had begun on the Woodstock–Port Dover Railway line. However, after several years the company went bankrupt and the project was abandoned, but not before a railway bridge had been erected across the Lynn. On this bridge the Fenwick Rifle Company drilled in the summer evenings. This bridge remained for many years until it rotted away. In 1875 the Woodstock–Port Dover Railway project was revived and the first train was run from Simcoe to Port Dover in 1875. However, the line took a different route and the old bridge was never needed.

The following report in the *Norfolk Messenger*, Thursday Oct. 5, 1854, gives some information about the railway line being built. The write-up was taken from the *Woodstock Gazetter* and is entitled:

THE WOODSTOCK & LAKE ERIE RAILWAYS

The correspondent tells about going over the rail-bed and seeing the work that had progressed up-to-date and he was quite favourable as to what had taken place. He talks about work in Simcoe, and I quote:
"About Simcoe the work is progressing very actively under Messrs. Martin, Zimmerman and Smythe and Mr. McBean the contractors, and this in the face of some very difficult cuttings. These cuttings in one or two places are from 20 to 25 feet deep through a clay almost as hard as rock. So much so that blasting powder is used for its dislodgement."

This photo of the old Railway Bridge gives a good view of the Tannery at the north-east corner.

Looking north on Lynn River from south of Argyle Street Bridge — circa 1867

The support for the carriage bridge which crossed the Lynn just north of the Railway Line can be seen under the first bridge.

The Tannery was a busy place for many years. An advertisement appearing in O. L. Fuller Business Directory for Norfolk County 1865 and 1866, states:
R. W. Weston Manufacturer and Dealer in all kinds of leather.
Foot of Argyle Street, Simcoe, Canada West
"A large assortment of leather of the best quality always on hand at the lowest prices. Hides tanned on shares."

In the *Long Point Advocate*, December 7, 1844 we read:

TANNERY

"The subscriber, having purchased the Tannery lately occupied by L. L. Douglas, begs respectfully to inform the inhabitants of Simcoe and its vicinity that he has on hand the following articles of superior quality and will dispose of them as cheap as they can be procured at any other establishment: *Calf skins, sole, upper and harnessed leather; hides or bark taken in exchange for leather or boots and shoes.*"
Signed: William Weston, Simcoe
March 28, 1844.

The Norfolk Golf & Country Club

The original site of the club house at the Norfolk Golf and Country Club was on the knoll that overlooks the present first green. This is on the south-west side of the present golf course, the photographer was looking south-west.

The main factory and office building of the Brook Woollen Company located on Victoria Street can be seen to the left.

The following article in the British Canadian, April 25, 1900, tells about the construction of this first club house building: "The Simcoe Golf Club are having a club house erected on their links by Messrs. Gunton & Son. The putting greens have been levelled and the links put in first class condition. The grounds are pleasantly situated on Lynnwood Farm and the club looks for a very successful season."

Following this original 30' × 30' building a new structure was erected in 1914 in the centre of the golf course.

Norfolk Golf & Country Club — circa 1905

Norfolk Golf & Country Club — circa 1922

Looking east and slightly north from the hill on which is located the first tee. This club house was opened on June 1st, 1914 and built at a cost of about $4,800. It included showers, baths and lockers in the basement level and, above, a large main room with a delightful old fireplace. There were also bridge rooms and a kitchen. The verandah was on both the south and west sides of the building and gave a very good view of the town and part of the Golf Course.

Tobogganing has always been a favourite winter pastime at the Country Club and apparently the early 20's was no exception.

This photo is looking south-easterly towards the south-west corner of the club house. The lawn bowling green was added in 1922 and the Lawn Bowling Club remained here until 1945 when they moved to their new location between Norfolk and Kent Streets on the south-west bank of Lake George.

Austin & Shand Garage, on the north side of Sydenham Street — circa 1916

South side of Sydenham Street, Oct. 18, 1961, looking south-west. The photo shows all that remains of the Canadian Tire Store which was destroyed by fire the night before. The firemen are still standing by, ready to extinguish any stubborn embers. Following the fire a new modern store was erected which stayed at this site until late in 1977 when the Canadian Tire Store moved into Simcoe's New Shopping Mall on No. 3 Highway East.

The first auto dealership in Simcoe was that of Austin and Shand. They obtained a franchise in 1913 to sell Chevrolets and the dealership was located at 37 Sydenham Street in the building now occupied by The Norfolk Recreation.

The following ad appeared in the *Simcoe Reformer* April 12, 1917, and gives some idea of car prices at that time:

McLAUGHLIN AUTOMOBILES

"The famous valve-in-head motors, fours and sixes. The classiest and most up-to-date cars on the market. Positively the best dollar for dollar value in the trade. Prices range from $910.00 to $1,900.00 with the most complete and up-to-the-minute equipment with every car."

"Ask for a catalogue. Better still, make an appointment for a demonstration. You owe it to yourself to make a comparison of the wonderful unexcelled value of McLaughlin cars."

CARS FOR HIRE, LICENSED DRIVERS.

Austin & Shand, Simcoe Garage,
Phones 301 & 78, Simcoe.

East side of Culver Street — circa 1935. The top photograph shows the pickling vats of Lealand Pickle Factory. The Lealand Company was established about 1895 on Culver Street by G. W. Lea. For years, until the disastrous fire of July 30, 1951, the company produced and distributed a very popular brand of pickle. The main office of the plant was located on the east side of Culver Street about half-way between Sydenham and Water Streets.

The pickles were distributed throughout the country by their own fleet of tractor-trailers.

The photograph at the bottom shows the vegetable receiving and grading sheds of the Lealand Pickle Company. The pickling vats can be seen in the background, at right.

This photo was taken from the *Simcoe & Norfolk County Old Boy's Reunion Book*. It shows a way of life long since past, but nevertheless a function of vital importance to every community.

Following are a few quotations from the above book:

"The mills were built on land granted by the Crown to Aaron Culver on July 17th, 1801. A saw mill was first erected on the site. The date of the building of the grist mill is not known. But on June 1st, 1830, Aaron Culver leased the grist mill, saw mill, frame house and garden to Duncan Campbell for ten years."

"On April 25th, 1844, Jas. W. Ritchie, Nathan C. Ford and David F. Jones purchased the mill and thereafter Mr. Ford remained owner of it for over 40 years."

"The mill burned in 1866 and was rebuilt by Ritchie & Ford. It was burned again in 1897 and rebuilt the same year. It was never wholly burned, however, and the present foundation is that originally laid."

The mill later became known as "The Quance Mill" and during the 1950's 60's and 70's it was used as a storage warehouse. If the 1977 plans of the Simcoe Little Theatre (for converting the old structure into a theatre) are brought to fruition, this historical site will again serve a useful purpose.

An advertisement in the *Simcoe Reformer*, April 10, 1924 stated:
"Farmers! We have a limited quantity of ground white wheat screenings; same as we offered several months ago. These are high grade @ $1.35 per cwt. A better value than shorts. Come in and see them."
Quance Bros., Simcoe Plant,
Mill Pond Street, Phone 62

East side of Pond Street — circa 1885, looking north-east from the foot of Water Street towards the Simcoe Mills.

Ritchie-Ford distillery, south side of Water Street at River Lynn — circa 1860

The Old Ritchie-Ford Distillery stood on the south side of Water Street. This was long before Pond Street was ever completed through to Victoria Street.

The photographer in this rare photo of the early 1860's, was standing on the west bank of the Lynn River, right at the base of Water Street. The picture is looking south towards the distillery and along the west bank of the Lynn River. Ritchie & Ford were a big business employing many men at their several locations. They also employed many teamsters to carry the liquor and grain to the Port Dover dock.

The Brook Woollen Company, south side Victoria Street — circa 1890

Looking south-west from the hill on the north side of Victoria Street, just east of the present bridge, the photo shows the Brook Woollen Company of Simcoe Limited. This company dates back to 1864 when Mr. Joseph Brook ran a carding mill at Lynn Valley.

In 1882 he established a mill on the south side of Victoria Street to manufacture worsted yarns; however, that building was destroyed by fire in 1887. The operation was re-established in 1888 when these two buildings were erected. By 1918 many additional buildings had been erected at the site.

An article in the *Simcoe Reformer*, July 31, 1924, gives some idea of the size of the company by that time:
"The Brook Woollen Company may be said to be the premier industry of Simcoe. It grew out of a mill started at Lynn Valley in 1864 and today employs 150 hands and pays out in wages $2,600.00 every week. The Company now has in continuous operation 40 looms and operates the plant fulltime and a portion of it night and day."

The Brook Woollen Company — circa 1940

This aerial view of The Brook Woollen Company Limited is looking south. The Victoria Street Bridge and Lynn River can be seen on the west side of the plant and the old L.E. & N. Railway tracks on the east side. This photo shows the plant at the peak of its operation in the 1930's and 40's.

The following excerpt is found in the *Simcoe Reformer's* Centennial edition, January 5, 1978:

"The business was re-established in 1888 at the present site by Joseph Brook and George H. Luscombe. While most of the wool was imported from Australia and New Zealand, local farmers still brought in wagon loads of their own wool and were reimbursed with cloth or blankets. A steam generator at the plant not only ran the mill but supplied electric power for the arc system in Simcoe."

"The number of employees grew from about 150 to nearly 300 during the war years and the company geared up production of shirting and battle-dress for the Army and Air Force, badge cloth, naval cap cloth, white flannel and uniform material for cadets."

"The looms were finally shut down in 1975. However, the family-owned business is now engaged in the retail sale of textiles, upholstery fabric, blankets, yarns and unfinished furniture."

The predecessor of The Brook Woollen Company of Simcoe Limited was a frame carding mill located in Lynn Valley. The mill was apparently on the north-east side of the river, north of the Concession Road between Concessions III and IV of Woodhouse. It was just south and east of the Grist Mill which stood on the south-west bank of the river.

The *British Canadian*, September 21, 1864, offered this information about the company:

"MILL PROPERTY FOR SALE"
"The subscriber wishing to return to England the coming summer, offers for sale his Mill Property, comprising GRIST MILL, SAW MILL, and small WOOLEN FACTORY, together with a good Brick Residence, and 45 Acres of Land. In the Grist Mill there are two run of burr stones and merchant bolts, with the necessary machinery for custom work; in the saw mill, one muley saw, with lath machinery; in the factory, the necessary machinery for custom work; all driven by a good stream of water, with dam and mills in good repair. The above property is situated in the Township of Woodhouse, 2½ miles from Simcoe, in the County of Norfolk, C.S., and known as the River Lynn Mills. For particulars, apply to the proprietor on the premises, or by letter, pre-paid, Simcoe P.O."
Alfred Ades, River Lynn Mills, 30th March, 1864.

And on April 2, 1866, this advertisement appeared in the *Simcoe Reformer*:

NO SHODDY, but the BEST home-made cloth.
"The scribers are manufacturing at their Carding Mills, River Lynn, the very best of home-made ALL WOOL CLOTHS and FLANNELS, which they are prepared to sell as cheap as the shoddy offered for sale in the stores. Their machinery being adapted for the exclusive manufacture of all-wool goods, they are enabled to offer great inducements. The patronage of the inhabitants of the vicinity is respectfully solicited. Entire satisfaction guaranteed."

"Carding, Spinning, and Fulling, and cloth manufactured by the yard, at the lowest cash prices."
R. Brook & Son.
Woodhouse, April 2, 1866.

Carding Mill of Joseph Brook — circa 1866, from a painting by W. E. Cantelon, looking north-west. The mill pond would be several hundred yards behind the mill.

The South-west corner of Norfolk & Stanley Streets — circa 1880

This picture, from a painting by W. E. Cantelon, is looking south along the west side of Norfolk Street from the Stanley Street corner. Few people know that at one time St. Paul's Church (Presbyterian) was located here. In fact, for a considerable time from about 1846 to about 1875, there were two Presbyterian Churches in Simcoe.

The early Presbyterian Church in Simcoe divided about 1846, forming St. Andrew's Church and The Free Church of Scotland. By 1850 St. Andrew's had built a new church on the gore of Dean and John Streets, now the St. James United Church Christian Education location.

The Free Church of Scotland worshipped for a time in the Gundry Church of the Free Will Baptists (11 Colborne Street South) until the above church was completed in 1869.

In 1875 the two churches re-united and worshipped in St. Andrew's Church until the present Presbyterian Church on Lot Street was dedicated on February 14, 1886.

The following report appeared in the *British Canadian*, Jan. 7, 1880:
"St. Paul's Presbyterian Church on Norfolk Street was sold last week to a Grange Hall. The congregation is going to erect a larger and more handsome church. We believe the new building is to be commenced this summer. Until it is finished, public worship will be held in St. Andrew's Church."

The Eva Brook Donly Museum

The Eva Brook Donly Museum, 109 Norfolk Street South, is one of Ontario's most important local history libraries. The following are excerpts from an article written by curator William Yeager in the *Simcoe Reformer* Centennial issue of January 5, 1978:

"By the time that Simcoe artist, Eva Brook Donly, willed her historic house on Norfolk Street South to the Town of Simcoe in 1941, there had long been an urgent need for room to grow. The large two-storey brick building, built ca. 1843-44 in the elegant Georgian or Loyalist style, had been one of Simcoe's oldest and most beautiful structures, home to two generations of the Mulkins family (a father and son as the Town's second and third postmasters). The exterior had remained virtually unchanged for a century of use, and the large attractive rooms inside provided an ideal setting for antique furnishings and display cases."

"In 1967 a large and modern

East side of Norfolk Street South — circa 1965

Centennial Gallery in back provided flexible exhibit areas and an archival vault, and a few years later a large-scale renovation of the old house brought new life and color to the original site."

"No matter how the Town of Simcoe and the surrounding countryside change in years to come, there will always be reminders left behind at the Eva Brook Donly Museum to show future generations an impression of what life was like in each period of the community's past."

NEW
Stove and Tin Store.

Chadwick, Ansley & Co.

Have on hand a large stock of

Cooking, Parlor & Box

STOVES!!

Well and Cistern PUMPS,

And a general assortment of

PLAIN AND APANNED TIN,

Copper, and Sheet-Iron

Ware, in the BRICK STORE on PEEL-ST. two doors west of Norfolk-street.

An inspection of the stock, which will be sold as

CHEAP AS THE CHEAPEST,

Is respectfully invited.

☞ EAVETROUGHING ☜

Attended to promptly.

THE BEST COAL OIL

Always on hand.

Simcoe, Nov. 16th, 1864.   133

Looking west on Peel Street from Norfolk Street — circa 1865. This rare photo of Peel Street was taken not too many years after the new Court House had been completed.

In 1868 Perry, Swinton & Company had a grocery store on the north-west corner of Norfolk and Peel Streets.

The small frame building just west of Perry and Swinton's was a boots and shoe store.

The sign over the next building reads 'stoves', marking the stove and tin store of Chadwick, Ansley & Company. A copy of their ad from the *Norfolk Reformer*, July 27, 1865, is reproduced on the left.

Next we have the grocery store of Fred S. Lansdell, who was a grocer in town for many years.

Looking up the south side of Peel Street can be seen part of the old Ritchie Ford Store on the south-west corner of Norfolk and Peel Streets, mentioned earlier in this book. The name plate for M. R. Steel, Saddler, can be seen half-way through the block.

Farther up the street is the barber pole of George W. Smith, whose ad in the *Norfolk Reformer*, July 27th, 1865, appeared as follows:

"SOMETHING NEW"

"Geo. W. Smith, Barber, Hairdresser, and Clothes Cleaner, begs to inform the public that he has a new article for shampooing the head, and has also procured new and superior materials for cleaning tweeds, broadcloths, etc. Orders will be promptly attended to at his shop, on the South side of Peel Street."

Simcoe, July 27th, 1864.

This photo, looking west from the roof of the Kindy Building (south-west corner of Peel & Norfolk Streets), was taken by the late John Rutherford, circa 1900. The Presbyterian Church can be seen in the background.

The following account of Peel Street is taken from Lewis Brown's *History of Simcoe 1829-1929*:

"Coming up Peel Street, on the north-west corner we find a large three-storey frame structure. In this there was a planing mill, cabinet shop and general woodwork's department. Many hands were employed."

The building was built by William Collins who turned the business over to Misner and Kendall who ran it for many years, followed by A. M. Best who later sold to Henry Hoffmann. It burned on February 7, 1904.

Following are just a few of the many advertisements and write-ups that appeared in the *British Canadian* over the years, telling us part of the story of this once industrious enterprise.

JANUARY 1, 1896 — "Mrs. A. M. Best will continue to carry on the furniture and undertaking business lately conducted by her deceased husband. The stock is large and well assorted in dining, drawing and bedroom furniture. The undertaking department will be in charge of a funeral director of 20 years' experience. Satisfaction guaranteed."

MARCH 2, 1887 —
> Misner & Kendall, Cabinet Makers,
> Upholsterers & Undertakers, Simcoe.

"A large quantity of all kinds of furniture kept in stock, or made-to-order on short notice. Repairing prompty attended to. Picture framing and all kinds of turning and planing executed. A large stock of coffins, caskets, etc., kept in stock and will be furnished on an hour's notice — night or day. Shop and warerooms corner of Kent and Peel Streets, Simcoe."

FEBRUARY 10, 1904 —
"FLOOD AND FIRE IN SIMCOE"

"Sunday was an exciting day in town between the elements water and fire, which are so usable for the comfort of humanity when under control but when uncontrollable, are destructive and tyrannical masters."

"About eleven o'clock at night, fire broke out in the large three-storey frame building on the north-west corner of Peel and Kent Streets occupied by Mr. Henry Hoffmann as a furniture and undertaking store. A raging wind fanned the flames and

South side of Peel Street — circa 1910. The photographer was standing on the north side of Peel Street, just west of Norfolk Street, looking south-east towards the south-west corner of Norfolk and Peel Streets (Kindy Building). The sign over the door in the far background advertises the Cockshutt Plow. The Bank of Commerce was located in the corner of The Kindy Block and Thos. R. Nelles, Insurance Agent, in the first office west of Norfolk Street.

made a terrific fire and none of its valuable contents could be saved. The Wells Block on the east, residences of Mrs. Walsh on the south, and of Mr. Berry on the north, were on fire several times and it required great exertions on the part of the firemen and citizens to save these places from complete destruction. As it was, the offices of Dr. Grassett and Mr. Baxter in the Wells Block with their contents were badly damaged. The heat was so intense that plate glass fronts were smashed in the offices of Tisdale, Tisdale and Reid, and the Town Clerk and the central office of the Bell Telephone in the Landon Block."

FEBRUARY 24, 1904 — "It is said Simcoe is to have a new Government Building. The Dominion Government has purchased from the Kendall Estate the vacant corner lot on Kent and Peel Streets where Hoffmann's Furniture Store stood and intends having a Post Office and Customs House erected on it during the coming summer. The location is an excellent one."

Simcoe's "OLD" Post Office

When this photograph was taken, circa 1909, Simcoe's New Post Office was nearing completion. The architect was L. D. Barber and the general contractors were Schulz Bros. of Brantford.

The following article appeared in the *Simcoe Reformer*, Thursday, January 20, 1910:

"Simcoe's New Government Building — It is expected that this issue of The Reformer will tomorrow (Friday) morning be delivered to its Simcoe subscribers from the new Post Office. People said it was too low. People, unacquainted with the modern trend in the architecture of public and semi-public buildings, noticed it had no tower, no clock, no variety of bright coloring, condemned it hastily. But the building has grown on people. Its straight dignified lines, its self-evident solidity appeals to one, the more it is examined. The Canadian stone harmonizes well with the warm tone of the Roman buff brick. The building has been little over two years in construction, the contract having been let in the Autumn of 1907."

This Post Office was, for many years, considered one of the most modern in Ontario. It was taken over by the Town of Simcoe in 1956 for the Town Offices and Council Chambers when the new Post Office was built at the north-west corner of Union and Norfolk Streets.

In 1977 the Town Council moved to new chambers in the recently restored "Old Courthouse" on Governor Simcoe Square; whereupon the local branch of the Bank of Montreal temporarily transferred its operations to this, the "Old Post Office", until their own premises on Norfolk Street South could be rebuilt.

The "Old Post Office", 1958, sporting in big letters "TOWN OF SIMCOE", above the centre windows.

South side of Peel Street — circa 1905

The photographer was standing on the north side of Peel Street about half way between Kent and Colborne Streets.

On the extreme left can be seen the C. A. Chadwick barn, where for many years the Chadwick Livery was run — this is now No. 50 Peel Street.

The small house was the home of a Mrs. Johnson, the mother of the late Henry Johnson and grandmother of the late Enid Johnson, two of Simcoe's foremost historians. Mrs. Johnson was a dressmaker.

The billboards are advertising G.HALL'S SPECTACLE, *The Holy City or the Way of the Cross* — to be shown at the Norfolk Opera House. Several other large Real Estate Posters and Auction Posters are tacked to the wall.

Simcoe's Free Library or Public Library and Reading Rooms were located at 58 Peel Street until the new library appeared at Argyle Street and Lynnwood Avenue in 1912.

Frank Pierce ran a printing shop at 60 Peel Street and above was Mabee's Hall owned by Peter Mabee, an auctioneer who lived around the corner at 55 Colborne Street South. This hall was used for dances and parties, etc., for many years.

An amusing story of Peel Street appeared in the *British Canadian*, August 19, 1891:

"On Saturday forenoon Peel Street was the scene of an exciting runaway, connected with which there was an unusual occurrence. A span of young horses, attached to a covered buggy, belonging to Mr. Anson Austin of Woodhouse, were left for a moment untied, opposite the Free Library. The horses took fright at something and dashed down Peel Street missing a number of vehicles which were on it, crossed Mr. Beaupre's vacant lots south of the Norfolk House, went through the fence on the east side — leaving the buggy — and ran into the kitchen at Mrs. Harding's Boarding House. Both the horses went through the door and were found in the kitchen beside the cooking stove. The cook was absent, having hastily retired seeing a couple of such unwelcome visitors. No damage was done in the kitchen and luckily the horses were unhurt. The damage to the buggy was slight. Altogether, it was a luck runaway and created a hearty laugh to see the horses in the kitchen inspecting what had been prepared for the boarders' dinner. Boarding house hogs and jack-asses we have read of but this is the first instance recorded of boarding house horses creating a sensation."

South-east corner of Peel & Colborne Streets — circa 1905, looking east along the south side of Peel. The corner building was erected in 1877 by John H. Ansley who for years was in partnership with T. R. Slaght, Barristers & Attorneys-At-Law. On the second floor were the club rooms of The Young Liberal Club.

Dean's Hotel, north-east corner of Colborne and Peel Streets — circa 1930

This building was located on the north-east corner of Colborne and Peel Streets. It was originally built about 1836 and was used as a Rectory for the Trinity Anglican Church. Afterwards it was converted to a hotel by a Mr. Shepherd. Later it came into the hands of Miel Dean. The hotel business remained here until about 1905 when the licence was taken away from the house because of the movement on the part of the temperance people to reduce the number of hotels and liquor shops in towns and cities.

From this time on, business fell off rapidly and finally the building was turned into a rooming house on the upper floors and mercantile shops on the lower floor.

The photographer was standing on the corner of Court and Colborne Streets looking north-easterly. The front of the building faces Colborne Street. This picture was given to the author by Mr. "Alfie" Johnson who occupied the south-west corner of the building for many years running a shoe repair shop.

The old building was badly damaged by fire and water in the late 1930's and was demolished by the owner J. J. Miller.

South side of Peel Street, during the Simcoe Old Boy's Reunion, August, 1924. One sign in the window welcomes the "Old Boys to the Old Home Town", and the large poster is advertising a performance called "Springtime" at the Fair Grounds, Simcoe, August 5 to 7. Bunting and Union Jacks decorate the building. C. A. Chadwick & Son Funeral Directors, were located for many years at 60 Peel Street.

The Norfolk County Court House

This early view of the Court House, circa 1870, looking south from the south side of Lot Street, shows the old wooden fences and rail fences in quite a dilapidated state, contrasting considerably to the relatively new white brick walls of the building.

A few excerpts from the *Norfolk Reformer* of March 19, 1863 tell the story of the destruction of the original building.

"About ten o'clock yesterday morning we were startled to hear the cry "FIRE" and on looking out of our office windows we discovered that dense volumes of smoke were issuing from the court house. (The Reformer office was then located on Lot Street next door to where the St. Paul's Presbyterian Church now stands). . . .

On proceeding to the building we found that the upper part of the court house was fast filling with smoke and in five minutes it was impossible to remain in the upper storey. All efforts were now directed to saving the papers in the various offices of the court house and in a remarkably short time the whole roof was on fire and it was apparent that it would be impossible to save the structure. The attention of the people was then turned to the jail . . .

Just as the above was in type, another alarm of fire was sounded. The music hall on Norfolk Street and adjoining the Norfolk House was in flames. When first discovered, the smoke was issuing in thick clouds from the side of the building next to the Norfolk House and in about two minutes from the time of discovery the whole building was in flames. The destruction of the Norfolk House seemed to be inevitable and the furniture was removed with all possible speed."

Norfolk County Court House, circa 1880, west side of Colborne Street south. This is the only photo the author has ever seen which shows the front gate and iron fence which once enclosed the front yard of the Court House.

Norfolk County Court House, circa 1915, taken from the south-west corner of Colborne Street and Court Street, looking north-westerly towards the front of the Court House. This excellent view shows the fine old trees that once graced the front lawn of the Court House building. Notice the wall surrounding the Norfolk County Gaol Yard at the rear of the building.

The aerial view of the Court House, circa 1958, is looking west up Peel Street. The Registry Office can be seen on the right (North side) and the Crown Attorney's Office on the left.

Looking west from the Peel Street-Colborne Street intersection, this fine E. S. B. Moore photo, dated circa 1910, shows the former Crown Attorney's Office on the left, built in 1861 and which, for many years, housed the Law Offices of Kelly & Porter, Barristers, Solicitors of the Supreme Court, Notaries, etc. The Registry Office, on the right, was built in 1893 and remained at this location until 1972 when a new Administration of Justice Building was built on No. 3 Highway west of the Town. Notice the cannon in the centre of the front lawn, the windmill behind the chimney of the Court House, and also the stately old trees that adorned the Square at that time.

View of Simcoe from Court House — circa 1865

This general view of Simcoe looking north-west from the tower of the then new Court House building, was probably taken by Isaac Horning. It is possible that the photo was taken during construction in early 1864.

The central or Union School which was located north of Robinson and east of Queen Street (torn down in 1930 for the American Can Co.) is in the background. The school was built in 1858. Beyond the school at that time was all farming community. Later in 1881 in front of the school the Simcoe Canning Company was established. The railway line along Metcalfe Street appeared around 1875.

The property on the south-east corner of Peel and Colborne Streets was owned in 1851 by Dr. John F. Clarke whose office, a little cottage, stood on the corner and his fine brick residence to the south on Colborne Street is now No. 55. This building is still standing; however, an addition has been added to the front and it is now used as an office building, having been occupied for many years by the Norfolk Tuberculosis Association, Harold I. Pond Insurance Agencies, Dr. L. S. Mason. The Real Estate Office of George E. Pond was located in this building until 1977.

Behind the Clarke house can be seen the Chadwick Livery Stable and in the far background the old Ritchie-Ford Grist Mill; beyond that, the hills across the River Lynn. The large brick building is the Empire Block, north-east corner of Norfolk and Water Streets.

The photographer was standing in the tower of the Court House looking almost straight east, or possibly in the Tower of the original Anglican Church.

South side of Colborne Street S. — circa 1865

DR. CLARKE, L.M.B.,
Physician, Surgeon & Accoucheur
CORONER.
Office hours, 8 to 10 a.m; 4 to 5 and 7 to 9 p.m. Office Days, Tuesdays and Saturdays.
☞ All Professional attendance, Medicine and Prescriptions, CASH, except by SPECIAL AGREEMENT.
Simcoe, April 21st, 1869.   xvim6

This exceptionally fine early photo is looking south down Colborne Street from just south of Robinson Street. The occasion was the 1st of July Celebration of 1879 which was always a big event in Simcoe.

On the left (east side of Colborne Street) can be seen the Old Dean's Hotel and beyond that on the south-east corner of Peel and Colborne Streets the new law office building of John Ansley, which was completed in 1877. The I.O.O.F. rooms were located on the third floor at that time.

The mottoes on this group of arches read as follows:
"SIMCOE GREETS A CENTENNIAL REPUBLIC."
"WELCOME — OUR AMERICAN COUSINS"
"LOUISE & LORNE"

The 1st of July was always a big day in Simcoe during the Nineteenth Century. 1879 was no exception. At sunrise the boom of an exploding cannon started the 12th Birthday Celebrations of Canada. Many events had been planned and people by the thousands found their way to Simcoe from all the surrounding areas. Bands and parades covered all the main streets in the town. One of the big events was a foot race of some distance, contestants were entered from several localities; many dropped out before the finish and the final winner was a Simcoe man by the name of Brown. The Simcoe Firemen put on quite a display for the townsfolk.

From the *Simcoe Reformer*, Thursday, July 3, 1879, we find the following:

"Three arches had been erected in separate parts of the Town, of these the one which by unanimous consent bore off the palm was the one erected by the firemen on the corner of Robinson and Colborne Streets. This, through the efforts of the firemen had been completely covered with flags and mottoes, the central one of which was "The Firemen Welcome Their American Friends". The fire engines, a couple of hose reels, a hook and ladder cart and other firemen's weapons had been arranged around and upon the arch with very picturesque effect."

On the corner of Colborne and Peel Streets another arch had been erected. The lettering on this arch (see photo) was a subject of considerable amusement — "Welcome Louise and Lorne" being one of the mottoes. Why such a motto should be used to welcome the Americans being a query that none but the authors could answer."*

"The last arch was the one erected by the Simcoe LaCrosse Club on Norfolk Street between the Federal Bank and J. A. Lyons Store. This arch was neatly decorated with flags and bunting; the mottoes were especially worthy of remark. "Pennsylvania, the Key Stone State, Centre of the Thirteen". First and Fourth of July, the Natal Days of Two Self-Governing Countries".

* *The Marquis of Lorne was the Governor General in Canada from 1878 to 1883. Why this motto was displayed is still a mystery as he made no visit to Simcoe in 1879.*

Old Gundry Church, 11 Colborne Street S. — circa 1915

Looking south-east along the east side of Colborne Street from just past Robinson Street. This photo shows the Old Gundry Church at 11 Colborne Street South. The old stained-glass windows of the church can be seen in the north wall. This picture shows the building being converted to commercial uses. Notice the upper window on the front right is replacing the old arched type curved window common to church buildings.

In 1845, apparently, a meeting was called of the Baptist Church to ordain Dr. Erith for the work of the ministry which he had done. But several months later it was discovered that this same person was working under an assumed name; his real name being Johnathon Gundry. Mr. Gundry then resigned from the pastorate and shortly afterwards a motion was made for him to become a member of the church. However, this motion was rescinded and the following Sunday 35 members of the church asked for their letters of dismission, for the purpose of organizing a second Baptist Church. These people formed themselves into a second Baptist Church in Simcoe (known as the Freewill Baptists) and about 1850 they proceeded to erect a brick church on Colborne Street and called Reverend Mr. Gundry to the office of pastor. He continued to act as such until the time of his death which occurred in 1855. The members dropped back one by one to the first church until the two were re-united.

In 1868 the building was purchased by the New Connection Methodist who continued to use it for five or six years. After that, the building fell into the hands of private ownership and has been used over the years for various mercantile purposes.

The exact location of The Maple Lodge Academy has not been determined by the author. However because of the clarity of the picture and its extreme rarity, being a very early photo of outdoor Simcoe, it was felt important to include it in this pictorial history. W. E. Cantelon has painted this scene and his notes simply state "Maple Lodge Academy, Colborne Street".

From the *Norfolk Reformer*, August 10, 1865:

MAPLE LODGE ACADEMY

"The attention of our readers is directed to the advertisement of this institution. It will be seen that a change has been made in the management and that the Rev. J. G. Mulholland is now the superintendent of the school. The reverend gentleman's abilities as a teacher are too well known to need any commendation from us."

The advertisement on this page, appeared in the same issue of the *Norfolk Reformer*.

Maple Lodge Academy,
For YOUNG LADIES and Boys under the age of nine years,
SIMCOE, NORFOLK Co., C.W.,
Will be re-opened
On Saturday, August 19th.
For terms, &c., apply to the
Rev. JOHN G. MULHOLLAND, M.A.,
Principal.
Simcoe, August 7, 1865.   351-2

Hiller's Livery Stables, 18-20 Colborne Street South — circa 1897

Hiller's Livery

The building on the north-west corner of Lot and Colborne Streets was built in 1896 and in those early days was used as a Livery Stable.

A. Hiller was in the livery business in Simcoe for many years, occupying several different locations. The following excerpts from various issues of the *British Canadian* tell the story:

JUNE 12, 1889 — "Early on Sunday morning, the horse and buggy which conveys the night mail from Brantford to Simcoe arrived at the stable minus the driver. Archie Hiller took the mail to the Post Office and found that the mail had been changed at Bloomsburg so that if anything had happened to the driver, Thomas Hiller, it must have occurred after he left there. Archie at once started for Bloomsburg and found his brother a short distance this side of there, alright. The seat of the buggy having upset, through not being securely fastened, and the driver fell out and could not stop the horse."

JULY 10, 1889 — "Archie Hiller, who was burned out last Saturday morning, has removed his livery to Bommer's Stables."

JULY 10, 1889 —

Large Fire in Simcoe

"Last Saturday morning, between one and two o'clock, the people of our town were aroused by the clanging of the fire alarm. It looked for awhile that the whole of the business places on the north side of Robinson Street between Norfolk and Kent Streets were doomed. The livery of A. Hiller was destroyed."

SEPTEMBER 23, 1896 —

Another Big Fire in Simcoe

"*Over $10,000 worth of property burned.*"

"Simcoe has again been visited by an outbreak of fire which caused the destruction of three places of business. A House of Worship and a private residence and several other buildings were more or less destroyed. At a few minutes to two o'clock on Monday morning, the rear of Hiller's Livery Stable and Dr. Eaid's Sales and Boarding Stables was discovered on fire, and owing to the inflammable nature of the buildings and their contents, were in a few minutes a roaring mass of flames from which the heat was intense. From these buildings the flames spread to Hill's Livery and the Salvation Army Barracks on the north, and to Mr. Burt's dwelling on the west, also. The heat was almost overpowering and the blackened and scorched appearance of the Presbyterian Church, Mr. Robinson's residence, Royal Hotel Stables, Wark's Warehouse and Atkinson's plant shows what a narrow escape from destruction they had. We regret to say that the circumstances connected with the origin of the fire lead to the belief that it was the act of an incendiary."

OCTOBER 28, 1896 — The bricklayers are making good progress on Archie Hiller's new Livery Stable."

NOVEMBER 18, 1896 — "Archie Hiller will move his livery into his new premises on the corner of Lot and Colborne Streets this week."

Browne's Garage

Taken from the centre of Colborne Street, just north of Peel Street, looking northerly along the east side of Colborne. This photo shows the Browne's Garage and the Nu-Way Warehouse Food Market at 27-29 Colborne Street South.

The town and countryside were startled on the morning of June 4, 1936, when an explosion rocked buildings and shattered many plates of glass and the Browne's Service Station was badly damaged. Five persons were injured, several of them seriously and were confined to the Norfolk General Hospital for varying periods.

Below, the rear of the building, after the fire.

Browne's Garage and Nu-Way Food Market — circa 1936

The Mechanic's Arch on the occasion of Lord Dufferin's Visit to Simcoe, August 28, 1874

The Mechanic's Arch on Colborne and Peel Streets, was quite an impressive structure with several members of the Mechanic's Institute on hand displaying their various inventions.

On the north-west corner of Colborne and Robinson Streets, facing Colborne, was the paint shop of Allison and Osborne and the following ad from the *British Canadian*, September 9, 1874, gives some information about this firm:

ALLISON & OSBORNE, PAINTERS

"The above firm would beg leave to inform the inhabitants of Simcoe and vicinity that they have opened a shop on the corner of Colborne and Robinson Streets, opposite Babcock & Mathews Livery Stable where they are prepared to do House, Sign, Carriage and Ornamental Painting. Particular attention paid to Graining and imitation of all kinds of wood. Paper hanging done on the shortest notice."

Fireman's Arch, Dominion Day, July 1, 1879

This exceptionally fine photo is looking west up Robinson Street from about 100 feet east of Colborne Street.

The description of this elaborate arch prepared by the Firemen for the 1879 Dominion Day Celebration was given on page 124.

On the south side of Robinson Street can be seen Lawson Bros, Saddlers, located at 62-64 Robinson Street. This firm must have moved here about 1878 or early 1879 as their ad in the 1877 Norfolk-Haldimand Atlas indicates that at that time they were located at Kent and Peel Streets.

Across Colborne Street on the south-west corner of Colborne and Robinson, facing Colborne, can be seen the Livery Stable of Babcock & Mathews, a prominent livery sale and boarding stable firm at this location for many years.

Melbourne Hotel, west side of Robinson Street — circa 1905

This photo, looking north-east along the north side of Robinson Street, gives an excellent view of the Melbourne Hotel. The Royal Bank did not occupy the Kent Street-Robinson Street corner location until 1919; however, the photo does indicate a retail outlet at the time.

The round archway in the building at 47-49 Robinson Street was the entrance to the Melbourne Stables.

The predecessor of the Melbourne Hotel was the Old Mansion House. This building was the site of many a lively party and it was often here that teams and other groups would congregate to organize themselves for the upcoming season.

The picture below is from a painting by W. E. Cantelon of the old structure as no actual photographs have ever been seen.

The following write-up in the *British Canadian*, Wednesday, May 29, 1895, tells about the end of The Old Mansion House:

A COSTLY FIRE IN SIMCOE

"The Mansion House and eight buildings were burned and over twenty buildings damaged."

"At two o'clock last Friday morning the ringing of the alarm and the glare of fire in the heart of the town announced to the townspeople that the fire king was again ravaging property in their midst, and one of the most destructive fires that Simcoe has witnessed for many years was the consequence. At that hour flames were observed breaking through the roof of a barn belonging to James Cutting, and occupied by two of his tenants, J. D. Murdock and G. O. Werrett, and which was adjoining the barns of the Mansion House and Mr. Charles Sihler, forming a cluster of three wooden structures."

"The fire then attacked The Mansion House and spread so rapidly that a number of the inmates narrowly escaped with their lives, losing personal effects. Only a portion of the contents of the hotel could be got out. The heat from the burning hotel was intense, and Cutting's block and E. E. Collins and William Collins shops on the west, the row of buildings on the south side of Robinson Street, Mather's block and residence of J. B. McIntosh on the east side of Kent Street and the residence, tenement house and shop of C. Sihler on the west side of Kent Street were in jeopardy, some of them being on fire."

"The same night there was a narrow escape from another fire in the Mabee's block on Norfolk Street occupied by J. J. Harris, dealer in boots and shoes and Hayes & Company, druggists."

Mansion House — circa 1890

Looking west on Robinson Street, from Norfolk Street — Circa 1908

This horse and buggy day photo gives an excellent view straight up Robinson Street from the Norfolk Street centre-line.

The H. S. Falls Store in the north-west corner with the Battersby House next are the only buildings with signs. However there has been little change, especially along the second stories of any of the buildings on the south side of Robinson Street. Notice the early electric lights in the centre of the street.

The following article appeared in the *British Canadian* on September 21, 1887: "Last Saturday night the streets of Simcoe and a number of the principal business places of the town were lighted with electrical lamps and the large number of people assembled on the streets to see how they worked, showed that the public was taking a deep interest in their success."

The reason for the flags and bunting decorating the H. S. Fall's Store is not known for sure. However, it is thought that this may be the decorations celebrating the moving to the new store across the street. In the lower right hand corner a wooden barricade would indicate a building project on the north-east corner of the block.

The Victoria Block or Wallace Block as it has been known, has been occupied by many firms. Following the fire of 1874 which destroyed their store on the south-west corner of Peel and Norfolk Streets, the Ritchie-Ford Company moved into the Victoria Block shown above. Sometime in the 1880's they disposed of the business to George Jackson McKiee who continued there until 1891, selling to Harvey S. Falls.

The *British Canadian*, April 1, 1891, reported:

" A NEW FIRM IN SIMCOE"

"Mr. George J. McKiee's large stock of drygoods, carpets, clothing, millinery, etc., has been purchased by Mr. Harvey S. Falls who will continue the business in all its branches as heretofore."

Mr. Falls became associated with the Northway, Anderson & Company who had stores in St. Thomas and Hamilton — thus the name Northway, Anderson and Falls.

In 1912 the H. S. Fall's Store moved across the street to their new modern department store and the Victoria Block was used by Wallace W. Walsh for a

Intersection of Norfolk and Robinson Streets — circa 1945

number of years as a furniture establishment. Eventually Mr. Walsh moved diagonally across the street to the south-east corner of Norfolk and Argyle Streets and for a brief period of time the building was used by another furniture company, Small and Kaiser.

In 1931 F. W. Woolworth Company took over the location.

The photo on this page dates back to circa 1945. Traffic lights had been installed at the intersection of Norfolk and Robinson Streets by then. It gives an excellent view of the original Woolworth Building and the old Battersby House.

On July 31, 1952, an announcement was made by the Woolworth Firm that they had purchased the Wallace Building on the corner as well as the adjacent Battersby Hotel. At that time the Company occupied the ground floor of the Wallace Building with the Norfolk Children's Aid Society offices being on the second floor; Simcoe's Little Theatre Green Rooms were on the third floor.

In the far background can be seen the Strand Theatre on the north side of Robinson Street.

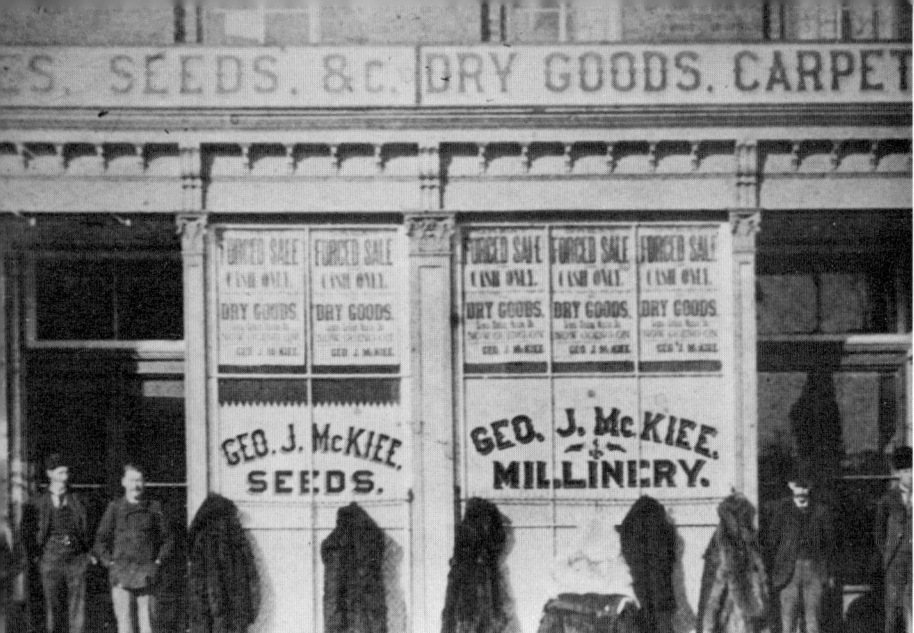

The George J. McKiee Dry Goods Store — circa 1890

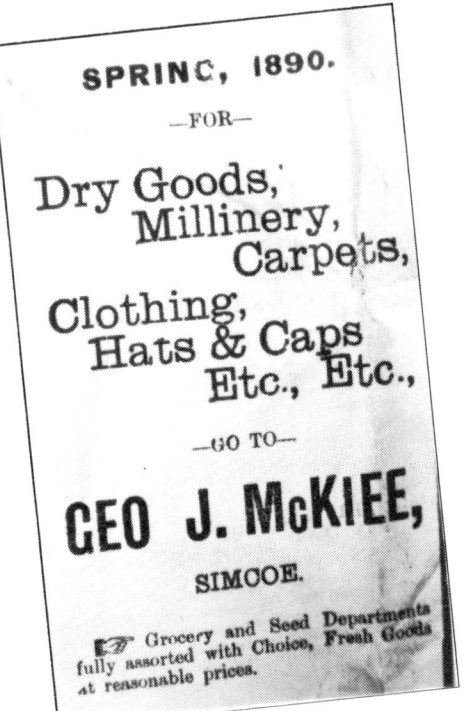

The George J. McKiee Dry Goods Store was located in the Victoria Block (Woolworth's) on the north-west corner of Robinson and Norfolk Streets.

In the *British Canadian*, May 11, 1887, we find the following:

"SOMETHING NEW IN SIMCOE"

"Although some sage remarked that 'there is nothing new under the sun', we can assure our readers there is something new in Simcoe."

"Our enterprising merchant, Mr. George J. McKiee has introduced into his establishment a novel and wonderful invention known as *The Rapid Transit System* for carrying money for sales from the salesman to the cashier and returning with the change. By its use, cash boys are dispensed with and the clerk is not required to leave his counter to make change. All he has to do is place the money in a small cup and touch a spring and it glides quickly along a wire to the cashier's desk and is immediately returned."

"When we visited the store on Saturday it was quite interesting to witness the working of the system and the rapid and thorough manner with which it facilitates business is at once apparent. As we do not possess the gift of the scientific American to describe the several parts of novel inventions, we will not attempt to give a description of it but would advise our readers to call on Mr. McKiee and have an ocular demonstation of its workings and at the same time they can procure some of the great bargains he is offering those who patronize him."

The photograph on the opposite page, by E. S. B. Moore, has the name "Mr. Falls" written in the corner of the original glass negative. It is not a photo of H. S. Falls but believed to be an interior view of his original store in the location of the present F. W. Woolworth block.

Notice the large Union Jacks on the table and the sign on the one bolt of cloth suggesting 10¢ (a yard?).

Possibly the strange looking metal apparatus above the man's head has something to do with the wonderful invention installed by the previous owner George J. McKiee, referred to as "The Rapid Transit System".

Interior of Falls Store, north-west corner Robinson and Norfolk Streets — circa 1903

Bar Room in the Battersby Hotel. The calendar on the wall reads either January 1905 or January 1908. Notice the old gas light and spitoon. Sign on the mirror says "Merry Christmas, Happy New Year". The photo was taken by Mr. E. S. B. Moore.

These photos were taken in front of the Battersby House during some type of cigar company promotion, circa 1905.

At one time there was a cigar company in Simcoe, as we learn from this advertisement in the *British Canadian*, June 19, 1895:

SIMCOE CIGAR FACTORY
John Mabee
"Wishes to notify the public that he has opened a Cigar Factory in Simcoe, and is prepared to furnish a high grade 5 cent cigar. The brand is 'THE MABEE CIGAR' which is stamped on the boxes and is manufactured of first class tobacco. Factory and residence at 13 Queen Street."

The event shown was probably a promotional skit sponsored by a competitive firm.

In all probability the clown band on the wagon are members of one of the early Simcoe groups. Possibly some day an article will be found in one of the early Simcoe newspapers telling the story of this event.

In the top picture the red and white barber shop pole of Russell McIntosh's can be seen on the left (#19 Robinson Street). The McIntosh Barber Shop was located on the north side of Robinson Street from 1888 to 1958. This photo also gives a good view of the old Battersby House which was torn down in 1954 to make way for the new Woolworth's building.

Calithumpian parade on Robinson Street, circa 1898, photographed by John Rutherford from the south side of Robinson Street, just west of Norfolk, looking north-west up Robinson Street. Notice the people on the balconies of the Battersby and Melbourne Hotels.

Calithumpian parades were common occurrences on holiday week-ends in Simcoe and from the *Simcoe Reformer*, Thursday, May 26, 1898, we find this headline: "Queen's Birthday — Right Royally Did We Celebrate It In This Town of Simcoe. The Grotesque Calithumpians Furnished Lots of Fun In The Morning"

The paper goes on to tell about the gala parade and the many exciting events of the day. Some of the floats in the parade represented "Happy Home", "Trick Elephants", "A Plantation Scene", "An Acrobatic Frog", and "A Klondyke Stage".

The day was overcast and some rain fell but the townsfolk turned out by the hundreds for the big celebrations.

Horse races and other contests were held in the afternoon. At night the men and ladies put on a lighted bicycle parade which was so interesting and colourful that it drew the attention of The Toronto Globe and Mail.

The Lea Store, as it was known, occupied the site of 22 Robinson Street (now Thornton's), around the turn of the century; the business later being taken over by Durham and Baker.

The following account appears in *Lewis Brown's History of Simcoe, 1829-1929:*
"About 1887 Mr. Lea purchased property on the south side of Robinson Street and built a brick block, moving his business to this new location. It only stood a little while, however, for in 1888 it was burned down. Mr. Lea immediately rebuilt and continued the business with but a slight interruption."

"On the new premises, in addition to what he had on Norfolk Street he added a new complete line of general groceries and went extensively into fruit, both foreign and domestic. The ice cream business was developed in an ice cream parlour fitted up, that did a brisk business. He had acquired a high reputation as a caterer and his services were ever in demand to cater at a dinner or supper."

"In connection with the bakery business, pastry was made a special line as it was necessary for its other departments. He did little in the manufacture of confectionery, except the making of home candy. Cigars, tobacco and pipes constituted another part of the business. Mrs. G. W. Lea managed the cooking and put up considerable quantities of pickles and preserved fruits. As time went on Mrs. Lea's pickles seemed to catch the public taste and she was occasionally asked for some. This demand became so apparent that Mr. Lea got hold of the idea that it might be well to extend the manufacture of pickles and to put them on the market."

This was the beginning of the Lealand Pickle Factory. Notice in the above photo that almost all goods for sale were housed behind glass counters and cupboards.

The Lea Store, 22 Robinson Street — circa 1920

Fred S. Chadwick Jewellery, 20 Robinson Street

Chadwick Jewellery started in the year 1893 and continued under the name Chadwick Jewellery until about 1960.

The business was started by Fred S. Chadwick and taken over by Sam Chadwick around 1923. About 1948 Loreen Yeager took over the business but sold it to Jack Eaid in 1958. The name 'Chadwick Jewellery' continued for about two years more.

The following amusing article was found in the *British Canadian*, Wednesday, December 16, 1903:
"Warning. I have been informed that two parties are selling watches in this County stating that I guarantee them which I do not, as I have no agents, and warn persons from purchasing."
Signed: S. F. Chadwick, Simcoe

The M. C. Brown building stood facing Robinson Street at the corner of Kent. To the east (No. 30 Robinson Street) can be seen Smith's Bakery. Little is known of this business. However, the following ads and articles from various issues of the *British Canadian* give considerable information regarding the corner building which stood here until 1896:

JULY 6, 1881 —

Go to Brown and Son, Simcoe
for

Fine Harness, Whips, Trunks, Valises, Satchels, Combs, Brushes, etc. We have a large and well assorted stock of summer horse clothing, fly nets, lapdusters, etc. The finest stock in the county. Cheap for cash.

Special attention paid to ordered work and repairing of all kinds.

FEBRUARY 23, 1887 —

M. C. Brown

Harness, Saddles, Fly Nets, Lap Dusters, Trunks, etc., The cheapest place in Norfolk. Come and see for yourself.

OCTOBER 19, 1887 — Mr. M. C. Brown has opened out in new and extensive premises on his old corner on Robinson and Kent Streets. The greater portion on the ground floor of his new building is used as a store and show room where a large and varied stock of harness, whips, valises, blankets, robes, trunks, etc. are displayed on shelves, stands and counters."

"The rear end of the same floor is used as a workshop where a number of skilled hands are constantly employed executing the orders entrusted to him by numerous customers. The building is a commodious one and the stock and premises will compare favourably with any establishment in the same line of business in Western Ontario. The Squire wishes to impress it on your mind that he has the cheapest shop in the county . . . See his new advertisement."

AUGUST 10, 1892 — "The public should note the following important facts concerning the harness establishment of Messrs M. C. Brown & Son. First, it is the largest retail harness business in Ontario with facilities and advantages for meeting the wants of the public as only a first class establishment can do."

M. C. Brown & Son, Harness Makers, south-east corner of Robinson and Kent Streets – circa 1875, form a painting by W. E. Cantelon.

E. H. Jackson Drug Store, 34 Robinson Street — circa 1900

E. H. Jackson, at 16 years of age, entered the drug trade as an apprentice in the store of Livingston & Company, then located at 32 Norfolk Street South (now Colonial Restaurant). Mr. Jackson became a chemist with this firm which later became Hayes & Livingston, then Hayes & Farlow, and finally Hayes & Company.

In 1896 the company purchased the above location but apparently did not move in until 1902. The following item appeared in the *British Canadian*, July 1, 1896:

HAYES & COMPANY, DRUGS, WALLPAPER, PAINTS, ETC.

"Having purchased the late M. C. Brown property on Robinson Street occupied as a harness shop, we propose converting it into the finest drug store in this part of Canada. We intend to rush the new building as fast as possible."

The first door south was the Harness Shop of William Abraham which had been here from around 1887, according to the following ad in the *British Canadian*, February 23, 1887: "William Abraham begs to announce to the inhabitants of Norfolk Street that he has removed his shop from Robinson Street to his premises on Kent Street, two doors south of M. C. Brown's where he will keep on hand or manufacture to order all kinds of harness and, being a practical workman, using only first class material, can guarantee a good job every time."

To the east of the drug store, at No. 30 Robinson Street, can be seen the grocery store of G. O. Werrett.

The Simcoe Armouries on the north-east corner of Robinson & Talbot Streets was built in 1913 and during the First Great War it was the home of "Norfolk's Own", the 133rd Battalion. The building was also used during the World War II by the 41st and 42nd Batteries Royal Canadian Artillery. It now houses the 56th Field Regiment including the 69th Field Battery. It is also used by the local Badminton Club. The top photo, circa 1913, shows the Armouries in the final stages of construction. The photo at left dates back to circa 1948. The truck in front belongs to Jackson's Bread Limited of Hamilton who operated a bakery in Simcoe for well over 30 years.

The Old Fire Hall

The Old Fire Hall was built in 1889. It faced Talbot Street with the Bell Tower on the south side.

The Simcoe Arena, on the west side of Talbot Street just north of Robinson, was built in 1948 on the same location as the Old Fire Hall and Bell Tower seen in the above photo. This picture, taken in 1907, shows the Fire Brigade and their equipment of this time. The photographer was standing in the centre of the Market Square Block, looking east toward the back of the fire hall building. The white house in the background was located on the east side of Talbot Street just north of the present Armouries.

Apparently the old Town bell was originally in a different location on the Market Square and was once the subject of a law-suit.

The following news items from various issues of the Norfolk Reformer tell this story:

MARCH 10, 1870 —
THE TOWN BELLS
"Jones, the maker of the bell in the Market Building has again sued the town for payment for the bell. The suit being entered in the County Court, Toronto, which is now sitting."

MARCH 17, 1870 — "The long pending suit respecting the town bell was decided on Saturday against the town. The council will therefore have the pleasure of paying for a bell that for all practical purposes, is perfectly useless to the town. What is to be done now? Is the bell to be used or are we to have one that can be heard a couple of blocks away from the market square? The town has suffered inconvenience enough and it is high time something should be done."

In subsequent issues of the *Reformer* we discovered that the town appealed this law-suit, but lost the law-suit in the Court of Appeal and had to pay not only the cost of the bell but also the cost of all the trials.

The *British Canadian* reported on October 2, 1889:
"The brick work on the fire hall on the market square has been completed and the tower has an imposing appearance. It is said the town bell is to be placed in it."

Simcoe Baptist Church

In the pioneer days of the Town of Simcoe, several denominations once worshipped in a single community building. This was a red frame structure which stood in the block bordered by Norfolk, Kent, Robinson and Peel Streets, and which not only served as a church, but as a school and as a public meeting hall.

The history of the First Baptist Church goes back to 1836 when at that time it was decided to organize a church in Simcoe and eventually erect their own building. It would appear that the first church was a frame building, approximately 40' × 60' and occupied about 1841. Because of water problems in the spring, the building was moved to the north-east corner of Colborne & Young Streets in the 1850's.

This chapel burned on July 24, 1867. After the fire, plans were made for a new church and on September 9th, 1869, the corner stone was laid on the original site at Talbot and Young Streets.

First Baptist Church under construction — circa 1869

First Baptist Church – circa 1910. This church stood in the same location as the present First Baptist Church on the north-west corner of Young and Talbot Streets. The front of the church faced Talbot Street. It burned on the afternoon of April 18th, 1913.

First Baptist Church – circa 1905

Simcoe Market

The first by-law for the establishing of a market in Simcoe was passed in 1868. However, in 1890, the Provincial Government passed a Market Act taking away from towns and cities most of their market privileges and restricting their power to control the sale of local produce within their corporation limits. This law put every rural market in the Province into a decline from which they have never been able to recover. The Simcoe Market dwindled considerably and then was discontinued entirely for about 15 years. However, in 1905, a completely new by-law within the scope of the Provincial Bill was passed by the town and the market re-opened until about 1915 when it again died because of considerable opposition from downtown merchants. However, it was opened again in 1928 and has continued to this day.

The following article appeared in the *British Canadian*, December 23, 1891: "Now that the new Market Building has been completed and the committee in charge are endeavouring to establish a good working market, the advantages of which are too well known to require argument, it behooves the people of the town to do all in their power to make its establishment a success. Let them take an interest in its working by patronizing it and inducing the farmers of the surrounding county to bring their produce to it for sale. Other towns have prosperous markets and why cannot Simcoe? Are drones and croakers to be allowed to stand in the way and prevent the progress of the town? Sweep them like cobwebs out of the way and let us have a good market in Simcoe. That is what we want and let us be determined that we will have nothing less."

The Market, north side of Robinson Street — circa 1940

Canadian Canners

North side of Robinson Street — circa 1912

South-east corner of Young and Metcalfe Streets — circa 1911

The Canadian Canners building (now Delmonte) in Simcoe, had their beginnings in 1881 when the Simcoe Canning Company was formed. The main principal in the company was William P. Innes. At first cans were made by hand, but by 1906 automatic can-making machinery was installed.

In 1920 The Simcoe Machine Shop (Canner's Machinery) was established to make the expensive canning machinery which had mostly been purchased abroad.

An article in the *British Canadian*, January 26, 1881, appeared as follows:
"A large quantity of brick is being delivered for building the new Canning Factory to be erected on the corner of Robinson and Metcalfe Streets opposite the residence of Mr. E. Mather. The building is to be 100' × 75', two-storeys high."

The Canning Company was an almost immediate success and by 1910 several additions and changes had been made to the original 75' × 100' brick structure.

About 1913 the original building was torn down and a new Process and Cooking building was under construction. This building was approximately 80' × 399' running lengthwise along Robinson Street. Behind this building a new storage and can factory building was constructed, about 75' × 275' in size.

The success of the original plant is evident from this write-up in the *British Canadian*, June 19, 1895:

SIMCOE CANNING COMPANY

"It is evident that goods produced by the Simcoe Canning Company are obtaining a world-wise reputation for their excellent qualities as Mr. W. P. Innes, the Manager, received on Friday a letter from Bombay, East India, asking for prices current for canned goods of various descriptions. It was signed by Abdool Rayom & Company. The letter was mailed in Bombay on 18th May and reached Simcoe on the morning of 14th June. This, beyond doubt, is the first letter of the kind ever received by any manufacturer in this district."

The photo on this page shows the construction workers building the storage warehouse and loading docks for the Canadian Canners in 1911. The building was located at the north end of the existing plant.

The north end of this building faced onto Young Street. In the 1970's this area of Young Street was closed off and deeded over to Delmonte (the owners of the Canadian Canners). New facilities have since been added to this end of the factory.

Ladies snipping beans in the work-building located at the back of the Canadian Canners off Young Street. Many people were hired by the Canners to snip the beans, some brought in by bus from other areas. Often the women would work at home in order to make a few extra cents for the family. The above photograph dates back to 1925.

This aerial view, photographed circa 1950, is looking east from above King Street. Robinson Street is on the right. On the north side of Robinson Street we see the plants of the American Can Company and Canadian Canners. Further up, at Talbot Street, the Arena and the Armouries. A thorough study of all the buildings in this photo, especially in the downtown area, reveals the many changes that have taken place. How many can you identify?

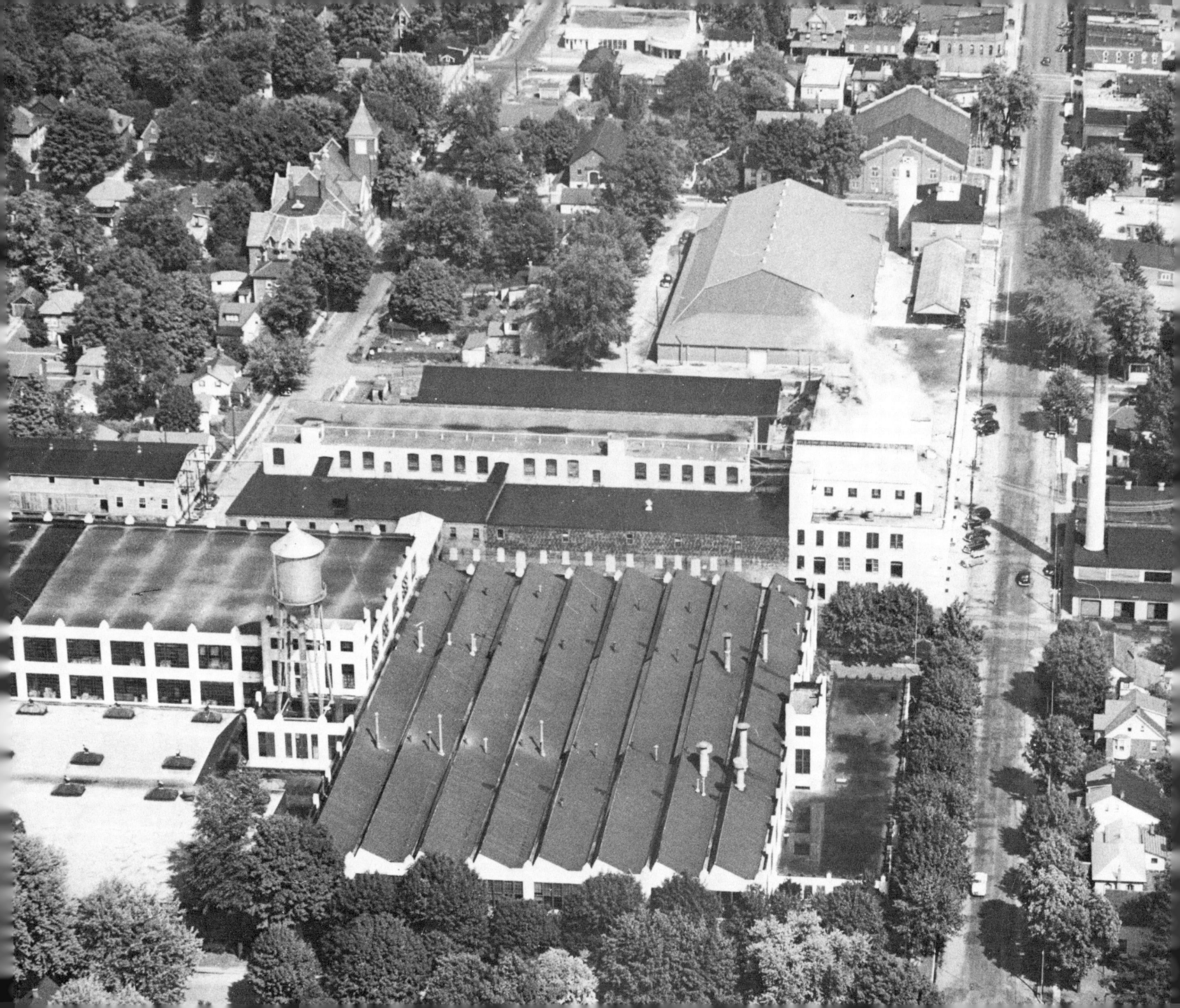

American Can Company, north side of Robinson Street — circa 1932

The American Can Company

This photograph of the new American Can Co. plant was taken from the south side of Robinson Street.

The American Can Company was built in 1929 and 1930 and since that time has been the leading employer within the Town. It annually ships millions of cans by rail and truck to the preserving factories of Canada.

Lewis Brown, whose *History of Simcoe* was completed in 1929, had this to say about the new company:

Looking east on Robinson Street — circa 1944

"Since this sketch was written, the Canadian Canners Can plant and the old Litho property have been sold to the American Can Company. At the same time the latter have purchased the Central School Property. They intend to erect a million-dollar plant on these two blocks and will employ 250 hands. It is the biggest industrial break Simcoe has had in many decades and fittingly enough comes on the 100th Anniversary of the Town's birth."

The American Can Company and the Canadian Canners are shown, in the photo on the right hand page, taken from the south side of Robinson Street, just west of Queen, looking east. Notice that Robinson Street, above Queen Street, was not curbed when this photo was taken.

A new one-storey addition to the American Can Company in 1977, filled the landscaped yard area beside the south-west section of the building.

Simcoe Lithographing Plant, north side of Robinson Street — circa 1913

Simcoe Litho Company

Built by the Canadian Canners, the Simcoe Litho Company was located just west of the Canners' factory on the corner of Queen Street, Metcalfe North and Robinson Street. Just north of this plant was the union or Central School. The Litho plant machinery was moved to Simcoe from London where it had been purchased. The offices were located in the west end of the plant with entrances off Queen Street North. The plant prepared all the paper labels for the soup and vegetable cans filled by the Canadian Canners. The Litho plant was completed in the autumn of 1912. Built of sand lime brick and cement, the plant was 87' × 278'.

The photographer was standing east of the railway tracks on the south side of Robinson Street, looking westerly and slightly north.

The following article appeared in the *Simcoe Reformer*, Thursday, February 8, 1917:

"Simcoe Litho wiped out. The most destructive fire that ever visited Simcoe. The splendid lithographing plant of the Dominion Canners falls victim to the flames. Eighty highly-paid artisans out of employment. Loss over a quarter million. Tons of labels burned."

This disastrous fire wiped out the lithographing branch of the Canadian Canners' industry and was quite a blow to the industrial expansion of Simcoe. Many of the highly skilled workers moved out of Simcoe following this fire.

Looking east from Queen Street at the ruins of the Simcoe Litho Company after the fire. The plant of the Canadian Canners can be seen in the background.

161

Metcalfe Street Station, looking north — circa 1910

Metcalfe Street Station

A large crowd of happy children and adults wait for the train to take them to Port Dover for a day picnicking and swimming. Notice the two hotel buses waiting for passengers.

Once a busy passenger station, the Metcalfe Street Station later became simply a freight station and more recently has been completely dismantled.

From the *Port Dover Maple Leaf*, June 20, 1890, the following item entitled "Simcoe Excursions":

"We are pleased to note the G.T.R. have again inaugurated the Thursday afternoon excursion from Simcoe to Dover which will be continued during the season. Trains will leave Simcoe at 1:15 p.m. and 6:00 p.m., returning leave Dover at 8:00 p.m. This is an admirable arrangement and no doubt hundreds of Simcoe citizens will be thus enabled to enjoy a cool lake breeze and fine bathing on the beach. The first excursion took place yesterday afternoon."

West & Peachey shipped their steam "Warping Alligator Tugs" by train from Metcalfe Street. To get them from their factory at the corner of Union and Norfolk Streets to the station, they embedded large posts into the verges of Union Street and the tugs winched themselves up the street and south along the railway tracks to the waiting flat cars.

As we read in the *British Canadian*, April 17, 1889:
"The Alligator Steam Tug just completed for Joseph Jackson, Esp., by West & Peachey, propelled itself up to the G.B. & L.E. Station on Saturday and was placed on a flat car for transportation to the lumber regions of Muskoka. It worked like a charm and we understand its owner was well pleased with its performance."

"Alligator Tug", its boilers still steaming, at Metcalfe Street Station — circa 1910

Union School, circa 1875, from an engraving in the Historical Atlas of Norfolk County, by H. R. Page Co., published 1877.

Union (Central) School

The Central Public School was located on the site now occupied by the American Can Company. The school was at the north end of the lot, on the corner of Metcalfe Street North and Kars Street. The front of the school faced east looking across the railway tracks and down Young Street. To the south of the school was the old Litho Company building. The Central School was torn down in 1930 to make way for the American Can Company.

The school was built in 1858 at a cost of $10,687 and was originally called the Union School. The contractors were Messrs. J. and G. Jackson. The old building housed all the schooling in Simcoe until 1893 when the High School was built. Two rooms were added to this school in 1885. In 1917 the Town had increased enough in size and had spread out enough that the Town Fathers erected the South Ward School on the corner of Agriculture and Brock Streets. In 1928 the North Ward School at Colborne, Windham and Main Streets, was built.

The photograph on the left was taken by E. S. B. Moore, circa 1910.

Union School west end of Young Street — circa 1865

The above photo of the old Union School was taken probably by Isaac Horning a few years after the bulding was erected. Notice that there are no trees around the front of the school.

The view is looking straight up Young Street with the photographer standing in the middle of Young Street, somewhat west of the corner of Talbot and Young Streets (Baptist Church).

When the Port Dover to Woodstock Railway project was completed in 1875 the tracks ran along the front of the Central School Building.

The following ad appeared in the *British Canadian*, September 21, 1864"

"Wanted for The Union School, Simcoe, Two Teachers, one for the Fifth Division at a salary of $300 per an., and one for the Fourth Division, at a salary of $250 per an., who are required to enter upon their duties on the 1st day of October."

"Applications must be sent to the Secretary of The Board on or before 28th of September."

John C. Mulholland,
  Secretary.
Simcoe, 20th September 1864.

The photo on the right shows the Old Central School being torn down in 1930. The American Can Company plant, almost completed, can be seen in the background.

Demolition of Central Public School — circa 1930

The "Titanic"

This photo is looking west from behind J. B. Jackson's on the north side of Union Street. This long two-storey barricks-type structure ran parallel to the railway track behind the present St. Mary's School. It was commonly referred to as "The Titanic." The building was used by the Canadian Canners during the 1st World War to house workers who had been brought in to work in the Canners during the harvest season.

J. B. Jackson Limited, west side of Union Street — circa 1907

This picture, showing the back of the J. B. Jackson plant (south-west corner), was taken by E. S. B. Moore, standing about 300 feet south of Union Street and east of the railway tracks. It was ordered by J. B. Jackson and apparently taken on October 31, 1907.

The following is quoted from *Lewis Brown's History of Simcoe 1829-1929*:

"One of the most flourishing Simcoe Industries of the present day (1929) is the cold storage, creamery, and ice cream plant conducted on Union Street by the J. B. Jackson Limited. The business was originally established by George H. Jackson as a coal and wood concern. In 1887 it was taken over by the late J. B. Jackson and largely extended by adding building supplies, oil and gasoline, eggs, cold storage, creamery, etc. Part of the present building was erected in 1900 for the storing of eggs being one of the first cold storages of its kind in Canada. The business was incorporated in 1919 and in 1922 an ice cream plant was added."

In 1933 the above plant and later additions were destroyed by fire. However, the company rebuilt the modern plant which is still in operation although under new ownership.

Norfolk General Hospital

Norfolk General Hospital, on the north side of West Street, was officially opened on May 20, 1925. This photo shows the townspeople gathering at the front entrance for the opening ceremony.

From the *Simcoe Reformer*, May 21, 1925, we read: "The Norfolk General Hospital, newest of Norfolk's public institutions and pride of the entire County, was officially opened yesterday afternoon, under most favourable circumstances. Glorious May weather, an assembly of more than two thousand expectant and enthusiastic people, the presence of His Honour Lieutenant-Governor Cockshutt, and above all the Hospital complete and beautiful in every aspect combined to make the opening day a landmark in the history of Norfolk County. It was truly a representative crowd that gathered in front of the main entrance at three o'clock and the ranks were appreciably swelled by the arrival of Simcoe's public school children fully five hundred strong."

The origin of the Norfolk General Hospital dates back to 1915 when by the will of James Allgeo more than $11,000.00 was left for establishing a public hospital in Simcoe.

In 1920 this fund was increased by a further $5,000 from the estate of William P. Innes. On Christmas Eve, 1923, Mr. W. L. Innes, the son of William P. Innes, donated the hospital site of 5 acres of land to the town. In February, 1924, a hospital fund-raising committee was set up by Town Council. By July 1924, three thousand subscribers had promised over $56,000 for the new hospital. Most of the credit for the tremendous response is attributed to Harry J. Brook who worked with untiring effort toward the final goal.

A contract was let in August of 1924 at a price of $50,800.00, the sod was turned in November, and the corner-stone laid on October 16th, 1924.

Shortly after the opening of the hospital, in 1925, the Simcoe Rotary Club raised $6,000.00 to provide a sunroom and an elevator.

By 1929 the hospital was accommodating 31 adults and 12 babies. By 1934 there were 36 adult beds as well as 4 cribs and 10 bassinets. Space was running out; an addition was becoming imperative. In 1937 the Simcoe and Delhi Kinsmen came to the rescue. A campaign netted over $31,000 to build a new addition. A donation of $5,000 from Mrs. A. W. Donly, grants by Town and County Councils, helped to bring this total up. A new wing was added and officially opened on June 10th, 1938. The new addition increased facilities to such an extent that no further addition was needed until after 1950 when plans were again put into motion for building.

Norfolk General Hospital, with sunroom and Kinsmen addition — circa 1945

The photo on the right was taken from the centre of Robinson Street at the intersection of Elgin Avenue — looking straight west into the front of the Norfolk General Hospital. At that time Elgin Avenue crossed Robinson Street and continued south to West Street. That portion of Elgin was closed off around 1972 when a new parking lot was erected. The original five acres of land donated to the hospital in 1923 by Wm. L. Innis seemed more than enough for all time. However, the additions of 1954, '67, and '75 left little room for future expansion.

In the 1930's, 40's and 50's the grounds were always kept in park-like condition enhanced by the Lighted Brick Entrance Gates at the end of Robinson Street.

The "McCall Nurse's Home" (photo at bottom), on the north side of Robinson Street, was donated to The Norfolk General Hospital in memory of the late Senator Alexander McCall by his family. It was officially opened in March of 1927 as a nurse's residence. In 1973 it was torn down to make room for the new Norfolk Hospital Nursing Home which was dedicated May 29, 1975.

This photo, looking north-west from the corner of Elgin and Robinson Streets, was taken circa 1950.

Norfolk General Hospital — circa 1945

In 1907 the Town constructed a public water supply for the benefit of its residents. Water of good quality was obtained from an infiltration gallery and pumping station immediately west of the Town on the north-east corner of West and Payne Street.

A distribution system of water mains was installed along the principal streets and fire hydrants were placed at strategic locations.

This picture shows the Waterworks Stand Pipe, looking north from West Street just east of Payne Street, circa 1910.

In 1962 an elevated steel water storage tank with a capacity of 500,000 gallons was erected just south of Howard Street.

Brick Works, Queen Street S. and South Drive — circa 1898

Charles Mason came to Simcoe in 1874. For a number of years he worked as a bricklayer in Port Ryerse and Port Dover. About 1883 he purchased the brick works on Queen Street South in Simcoe. For more than 40 years, Mr. Mason operated these brick yards, building it up into a thriving business. He made bricks for many years for the prominent buildings in Simcoe, including the Woollen Mill, Presbyterian Church, Melbourne House, Queen's Hotel, Fire Hall, Salvation Army Hall, Registry Office and many others.

Mr. Mason was most active in the Salvation Army and also in the Town's political affairs.

The above photo was taken from Queen Street on the south side at approximately South Drive looking north and slightly west. The Charles Mason home, now No. 210 Queen Street South, is at the right. Wood, for the baking of the bricks, can be seen against the storage shed.

The clay for manufacturing the brick came from the hills between Grove Street and South Drive; this is now the area of Stephen's Court.

The clay was formed into bricks, then put into the kilns for baking. After being baked they were placed on the drying racks seen in the main yard.

Norfolk County Fair, "Older Than Confederation", October 16, 1913

Norfolk County Fair

The Norfolk County Fair dates back to 1840, but it was not until 1869 that the present location on South Drive was purchased. The *Simcoe Reformer*, June 3, 1967, gives the following historical account:

"The year that Simcoe was incorporated as a Town, 1878, the Norfolk County Fair was already 38 years old, having started in 1840. The present location on South Drive, was purchased in 1869 from John Axford with additional land obtained later from Zebulon Landon, father of Monroe Landon, from whom more land was purchased in 1966."

"Some buildings were built at the time of the land purchase from Mr. Axford including a fine building topped by a dome and flag-staffed. This was completely destroyed by a fire on July 3, 1903. Until the permanent property was obtained in 1869 the fair was held at several different locations and under several different names, such as the Norfolk Union Fair, the Norfolk Union Exhibition and finally in 1907 the Norfolk County Fair."

"In 1886 the half mile track was proposed as well as the original grandstand."

The various buildings on the grounds have been moved from time to time for the many expansion programs that have taken place.

"The Crystal Palace", Norfolk County Fair (date unknown)

A brief article in the *British Canadian*, Wednesday, October 22, 1902, mentions The Crystal Palace:
"The main building, or Crystal Palace as it is popularly called, is one of the principal features of the show. The building as usual was literally packed with sight-seers and in the ladies' fancy work and coverlet departments the number of exhibits was in excess of that of last year. They were grand displays."

The fate of the main building or "Crystal Palace" is found in these headlines from the *Simcoe Reformer*, July 10, 1903:
"The sky to the south is no longer pierced by the dome and flagstaff surmounting the rather imposing main building of the NORFOLK UNION FAIR."

The write-up of this fire goes on to tell that it happened on the 3rd of July and was caused by lightning. The building was probably built around 1869.

The photograph on the right was taken from the grandstand area looking east, circa 1910. Notice the barns and picket fence along the east side of the grounds, and the fine residences of Norfolk Street in the background.

Brook's Dam, River Lynn — circa 1910

The Brook's Dam in the south end of Simcoe on the Lynn River, was built in 1905 to replace a previous dam which had washed out. The previous dam had been located some 500 feet north of the new structure. The dam was used to produce water power to run the machines for the Brook's Carding Mill which became the Simcoe Wool Stock Company. The firm carded wool and made yard, blankets, tweeds and other cloth for wholesale trade. This firm was the foundation company for the Brook Woollen Company Limited. This area is now part of the popular Brook's Conservation Park.

The following appeared in the *British Canadian*, March 28, 1900:

"On Tuesday noon of last week the dam at Brook's Shoddy Mill suddenly went out. The first the mill hands knew of it was when the machinery stopped. As this is used for the electric light station, the lights are being run from the Brook Woollen Mills. As it is impossible to rebuild the dam while the frost period exists, a steam engine has been placed in the works until the dam is rebuilt."

Yeager's horse barn and residence, west side of Norfolk Street South — circa 1910

The "Tastee Treat" on Norfolk Street South which opened in 1951, is on the site of "The Old Yeager Horse Farm." According to The Simcoe Reformer of January 5, 1978, this was once a 26-acre showplace devoted to prize-winning animals.

The picture is looking north-west from just south of the present Cherry Street (which would now run through the south end of the horse barn).

An amusing article of Aynsley Yeager, the owner and a very prominent man about town, was found in the *British Canadian* of June 14, 1916:

"Aynsley Yeager was found lying on the road unconscious in front of H. Groff's residence on Monday morning. His horse and wagon were standing near. He was placed in an auto and conveyed to Dr. Bowlby's office where he revived and was able to walk to the car after having some ugly bruises on the side of his face and head tended to. He was reported doing well the same evening. No one seems to have seen him fall from the wagon or to know the cause. Woodhouse has, however, a piece of roadway down there that vies with Norfolk Street in the matter of belying the name of "road". Maybe Mr. Yeager got seasick as many others are apt to do whether they drive over it fast or slow."

South-west side of Dean Street — circa 1860

This copy of a painting by W. E. Cantelon is looking north-west along Dean Street, from a few hundred feet south-east of the John Street gore.

Lewis Brown in his *History of Simcoe, 1829-1929*, tells us that the Presbyterians in Simcoe divided about 1846, forming St. Andrew's and The Free Church of Scotland:

"The members of the Free Church of Scotland about this time secured the use of the brick Chapel on the east side of Colborne Street, then the property of The Free Will Baptists (Gundry's Church). The St. Andrew's branch continued to worship in the grammar school until March 3rd, 1850, when their new church on the gore of Dean and John Streets, now the property of Senator McCall Estate, was dedicated. This was Simcoe's First Presbyterian Church."

North-east side of Dean Street — circa 1916

Dean Street is perhaps the most historically prominent residential street in Simcoe. It was on this street, in homes such as the one above, that many of the more influential families once lived.
In the foreground can be seen the horse-drawn dairy wagon of The Strathlynn Dairy.

The following ad found in the *British Canadian*, June 7, 1916, tells something about this popular business:

A SANITARY DAIRY

It is the desire of the Strathlynn Farms to give their customers the very best milk and cream that can be produced.

At considerable expense, they have recently rebuilt their Dairy House and installed the following machinery: — Milk and cream clarifier — Milk and cream cooler — Sanitary bottling machine — Steam turbine, bottle washer and sterilizer.

With the choice herd of dairy cows and excellent stable equipment, the milk and cream produced by the Strathlynn Farms is the very highest quality and being handled throughout in a sanitary manner, will be appreciated by all consumers who demand the best.

Inspection invited.

One of the more prominent homes in Simcoe for many years was that of Senator Alexander McCall. He was a successful lumber merchant and in 1908 was elected Conservative representative for the County of Norfolk to the House of Commons. In 1913 he was called to the Senate of Canada. In 1956 this old home on Dean Street was torn down to make way for The St. James' United Church Christian Education Centre.

East side of Colborne Street — circa 1915

Long referred to as "The Nelles Home", this gracious building still stands on the north-east corner of Stanley Street and Colborne Street. The building was purchased by Thomas R. Nelles, a successful real estate and insurance agent in the late 1800's. It remained as the private residence of the Nelles family until 1975 when it was sold to The Norfolk Association for the Mentally Retarded.

In January of 1977, the newly restored residence was opened to provide a stepping stone to independent living for A.R.C. Industries Trainees as full-time employees in the Community.

Methodist Church

According to Lewis Brown's *History of Simcoe, 1829-1929:* "The Methodist Church in Simcoe dates back to 1820. However, it was not until 1840 that they built their first church, a frame building on the same location as the present edifice stands. This building was replaced in 1860 by a new brick church which was destroyed by fire in the 1890's. The present church building with a large school room at the rear was built in 1897."

The *British Canadian*, November 18, 1896, had this to say about the new building:

"The contract for the New Methodist Church in this town was awarded to Mr. John Montgomery. The contract price is $9,475.00. The church will be larger than the old one; it will be 50' × 80' with a Sunday School room in the rear 50' × 50'.

The union of the Methodist Congregations and part of The Presbyterians in 1925, resulted in the formation of The United Church of Canada.

In 1957 St. James' built a new Christian Education Building on the Dean Street-John Street Gore, where once stood the St. Andrew's Presbyterian Kirk and later the home of Senator McCall.

The St. James' Manse on the north-west corner of Colborne and Stanley Streets was built in 1965.

This photograph dates back to circa 1910.

Trinity Anglican Church — circa 1875

Trinity Anglican Church

The history of Trinity Anglican Church goes back to about 1848, when in 1848 talk was first started about building a church. It would appear that the church was completed some time around 1850. Over the years the church was enlarged and added to from time to time, with a fairly large addition taking place in 1860.

The above photo is looking south from the intersection of Peel and Colborne Streets. It shows the church as it looked from 1860 to around 1882.

In 1882 all of the first structure north of the transepts was torn down and the church was completed as it now stands.

The Trinity Anglican Church in Simcoe is considered one of the most beautiful sacred edifices in the county. It is reported to have been modelled upon a parish church in old England.

The following write-up appeared in the *British Canadian*, October 25, 1882:

TRINITY CHURCH, SIMCOE

"Dedication, delightful weather, crowded congregations and highly interesting services."

On Sunday last, the 22nd inst., the new Trinity Church in this town situated on the corner of Colborne and Court Streets, was dedicated by the Lord Bishop of Huron, according to the rights and usages of the Church of England."

In the photograph on the left, by E. S. B. Moore, circa 1910, the corner of the old Crown Attorney's office can be seen on the right.

The Old Mud Church

This photo was taken from the Court House by Isaac Horning approximately 1861, and is looking straight north from the Court House. The small frame building stands just east of the present Presbyterian Church and was the office of the *Norfolk Reformer* in 1869.

In the background can be seen the historic Mud Church which was located on the south-west corner of Colborne and Young Streets. Lewis Brown in his *History of Simcoe 1829-1929*, mentions this old church:

"The front of the Church, built by the Congregationalists in 1843, faced Colborne Street. It was certainly not an attractive looking edifice when finished but very substantial, having been built from straw and clay bricks obtained from a vacant lot across the street."

"On top was placed a tall spire of tin or zinc or other bright material. It pierced the sky for some thirty or forty feet, running to a sharp point. On a clear day this could be seen from a long way off, and for more than 40 years it was the focal centre for anyone approaching the town from any direction."

In 1876 a mysterious fire took place in the Old Mud Church. However, it was not completely destroyed and stood deserted for quite some time.

In 1888 Colonel T. R. Atkinson, a one time mayor of Simcoe, purchased the site. The burned-out shell of the church was torn down and a new two-storey brick building was erected.

The Old Mud Church — circa 1860, from a painting by W. E. Cantelon, the view is looking east on Young Street from between Colborne and Talbot Streets.

Atkinson Marble Works — circa 1910

T. R. Atkinson purchased the site of the Old Mud Church in 1888 and became the proprietor of the Gore Marble and Granite Works which became one of the largest employers of skilled labour in the Town. Later the business name changed and the following ad appeared in the *British Canadian*, January 1, 1902:

THE ATKINSON MARBLE & GRANITE CO.

"Monuments, Head Stones, Furniture and Marble Works of all kinds designed and executed in the best style. We get our marble direct from the quarry. Our workmen are acknowledged to be first class. Also designs in Scotch Granite. A call solicited to examine work and compare prices. Near the corner of Colborne and Robinson Streets, Simcoe, Ontario."

The business was carried on by Colonel Atkinson's nephew and following his death, by P. O. Austin who purchased the plant from the Atkinson estate.

The main brick building still stands.

W. H. Abbey Co., east side of Colborne Street North — circa 1925

William H. Abbey Plumbing and Electrical business has been operating from 11 Colborne Street North from at least 1916. The following ad appeared in the *Simcoe Reformer*, November 16, 1916:
"Plumbing, Tinsmithing, Electric Wiring and Fixtures,
For promptness and first class workmanship see
    William H. Abbey, Telephone No. 42
      11 Colborne Street"
Over the years this long established firm has seen many changes — not only within their own business but within the community as a whole.

St. Paul's Presbyterian Church

St. Paul's Church was dedicated on February 14th, 1886. Rev. R. McRoll was the minister at the time.

In 1846 the Presbyterians had divided into St. Andrew's and The Free Church of Scotland. For a time each had their own place of worship. The Free Church at the corner of Norfolk and Stanley Streets and St. Andrew's in the Dean Street-John Street Gore. About 1876 the two churches reunited and worshipped in the Norfolk Street edifice. When that building was sold, around 1880, the congregation moved to St. Andrew's Church until the completion of St. Paul's in 1886. St. Paul's Manse was built in 1905.

The above photo was taken by Mr. E. S. B. Moore on November 26th, 1906. It was ordered by the Reverend Mr. Dey, minister of the church at that time.

The photographer was standing on the south-east corner of Talbot and Lot Streets, looking north-easterly.

We end our tour through Simcoe's past on the north-west corner of Colborne and Young Streets, not the busiest corner for commerce in the Town of Simcoe and not the site of a designated historical old building, but nevertheless a location ripe with the history of our community and now occupied by a long established family business connecting part of the 'then' with the 'now'.

From the Centennial issue of the *Simcoe Reformer*, January 5, 1978, we read:

"The oldest established furniture business in Simcoe under the same family proprietorship is MacGregor Furniture Limited at 54 Colborne Street North."

"Present owner of the business is Donald H. MacGregor whose father Howard MacGregor purchased what was then a funeral home and furniture store in 1926, from Joseph Coates, a well known local citizen and businessman. The funeral parlour was later moved to 96 Court Street in the building now occupied by George E. Pond Real Estate."

At one time there was a hotel at the above location known as the 'Life Henry Tavern', the proprietor's name being LIFE HENRY. Lewis Brown tells us that "it was at this place that the Americans used to have their headquarters when they came over to kidnap escaped negroe slaves. The practice was to come here and when they found an escaped slave, invite him to the Henry Hotel, there fill him with liquor, take him to Port Dover and, while in an intoxicated condition, put him on board ship and take him out in the lake."

So much for "The land of the free and the home of the brave. . ." and so much for the citizens of the town named after our first Lieutenant Governor whose first act of initiative was to abolish black slavery in Upper Canada.

H. MacGregor, 54 Colborne Street North — circa 1935

Epilogue

We have toured the town of yesteryear and have seen some of the achievements of Simconians over the past years. Perhaps it is good to pause occasionally and reflect on some of these physical reminders of the past.

The industrial expansion that is now taking place along the shores of Lake Erie will undoubtedly have a tremendous impact on the Simcoe scene in the years to come. We, and the younger generation now entering the working force, are faced with the responsibility of planning the way of life of future generations. We must remember that we can only learn from experiences of the past; progress is not necessarily tearing down and rebuilding something new; progress is not necessarily increasing our population at a specific rate of growth; progress is not necessarily greater take-home pay — but progress is anything that improves our way of life; it is improving our relationship with our fellow-man. We can only improve as we correct and build on our experiences of the past.

It is good, then, to retain and preserve some of the tangible things which our forefathers have left to us. They are the reminder that we are an on-going society. This is our heritage.

My Town — Simcoe

Not just a huddle of buildings and roof-tops,
    Not just a jungle of concrete and stone.
You are my haven, my refuge, my shelter,
    You are my heritage — you are my home!

I love your parkland, your trees and your houses,
    Your Carillon Tower with sweet ringing bells.
Men who have builded that others might follow
    Have builded a dream town where happiness dwells.

Here there's no strangers for here we are neighbours,
    Still just a "small town", no semblance of strife.
You are a beacon, a lode-star, an anchor,
    You draw me and hold me to your way of life.

Frances Bell Pond